Implementing Power BI®

in the

Enterprise

Dr Greg Low

SQL Down Under Pty Ltd

2

Implementing Power BI® in the Enterprise

Dr Greg Low
SQL Down Under Pty Ltd
@greglow

https://enterprisepowerbibook.sqldownunder.com

First edition June 2021
Power BI is a registered trademark of Microsoft Corporation

Cover Awesome image by the amazing **Pang Yuhao**
(c/- Unsplash https://unsplash.com/photos/OPwYu6nhWFc)

I have done my best to make this eBook as error free as possible at the time of publication, but I do not promise that it is error free or that anything we describe will work for you or continue to work for you. Every one of these technologies is a moving target. This eBook does not replace professional advice.

Note from the author:

I have worked with data for decades. This eBook is a compilation of the lessons I have learned when implementing Power BI based systems across a variety of organizations.

We intend to keep enhancing and upgrading this book. If you have feedback for it, please send that to enterprisepowerbibook@sqldownunder.com

About the Author Dr Greg Low

Greg is one of the better-known database consultants in the world. In addition to deep technical skills, Greg has experience with business and project management and is known for his pragmatic approach to solving issues. His skill levels at dealing with complex situations and his intricate knowledge of the industry have seen him cut through difficult problems.

Microsoft has specifically recognized his capabilities and appointed him to the Regional Director program. They describe it as consisting of "150 of the world's top technology visionaries chosen specifically for their proven cross-platform expertise, community leadership, and commitment to business results".

Greg leads a boutique data consultancy firm called SQL Down Under. His clients range from large tier-1 organizations to start-ups.

Greg is a long-term Data Platform MVP and considered one of the foremost consultants in the world on Microsoft data-related technologies. He has provided architectural guidance for some of the largest SQL Server implementations in the world and helped them to resolve complex issues. Greg was one of the two people first appointed as SQL Server Masters worldwide. Microsoft use him to train their own staff. He has worked with Power BI since before it was initially released.

A talented trainer and presenter, Greg is known for his ability to explain complex concepts with great clarity to people of all skill levels. He is regularly invited to present at top level tier-1 conferences around the world. Greg's SQL Down Under podcast has a regular audience of over 40,000 listeners.

Outside of work and family, Greg's current main passion is learning Mandarin Chinese, determined to learn to read, write, speak, and understand it clearly.

Training

Why train with us?

Training is a significant investment both in the out of pocket costs and in the time away from normal work. It's important to make that investment pay. SQL Down Under are master trainers. Our mentors are even called on by Microsoft when they want to train their own staff. You should do the same.

Why learn second-hand? SQL Down Under teaches many of the other trainers in the region. Get the right information, with deep insights, directly from the source. Greg Low is our principal mentor. He was the first SQL Server master, was chosen by Microsoft as an instructor in their Masters certification program, and has an active involvement with the product teams every day. You can find details about Greg here.

SQL Down Under offers premium public and private Microsoft SQL Server, Power BI, and other data-related training in Melbourne, Sydney, Canberra, and Brisbane, and on-demand online training that you can take right now.

Learn with an instructor

We offer two styles of instructor-led training: Online Live and Classroom Live. Both are led by an instructor. Both offer the same presentation, and hands-on lab work. The only thing that is different is where you attend from. With Online Live, you attend from your home or office, anywhere in the world. With Classroom Live, you attend from one of our classrooms.

NOTE: At present we are not scheduling Classroom Live courses due to COVID-19. These will return when possible.

Learn right now - online and on-demand!

If you'd like to learn right now, we have a range of online courses available. These courses have exactly the same content that you'd learn in our live courses, and they even offer the same hands-on lab work, and completion certificates. Learn right now !

Need to learn about data? SQL Down Under offer online on-demand courses that you can take whenever you want. We have many data-related courses.

You can learn with Greg right now!

We are rapidly expanding our list of courses.

Check us out now at https://training.sqldownunder.com

Need assistance with a project? Want help with the architectural design, or with getting a project back on track?

Contact https://sqldownunder.com to see how we can help.

Table of Contents

16

Introduction

What this book is and is not about

Thanks for reading this book. To make sure we are on the same page (pun intended), I would like to start by spelling out what this book is and is not about. This book is not an introduction to Power BI. It is also not a book that explains how to create the best visualizations in Power BI. In fact, it does not cover much about building reports.

This book is about putting a framework in place so that you can build great reports using Power BI. It is about all the things that you need to have in place to make it easy to build those great reports, and about doing that in a way that can work in enterprises. Power BI is an amazing tool that is so easy to get started with. But when it comes to making it fit into an enterprise way of thinking, some planning is needed. It is important to understand that Power BI was designed to

Awesome image by Jaredd Craig

appeal immediately to power users. It was not targeted at enterprise IT developers.

I see it a bit like I used to see Microsoft Access years ago. In the data community, the use of Access as a database is almost like a running joke as it is not really considered a database. Worse, many companies have challenges with data that has been spread across Access databases all over the organization in an uncontrolled way. I do not see Access that way. I was never a great fan of it, but I know that there are many applications today that would never have existed if the people who started them, were not able to use Access. It was an enabling technology that let ideas get off the ground.

Power BI today has a similar potential issue. It enables so many people to get data and reporting ideas started. For many people, that might also be all that has ever needed. Enterprises, though, can end up viewing this differently. Silos of data with varying quality and management are not going to be popular.

In this book, I will show you how I structure data models, how I stage and process the data, and how I secure it. I will also show you some techniques that I use to automate the process of building the data models.

There is no one right or wrong way to implement Power BI in an enterprise. In this book, I will tell you how I do it, and I have been implementing many successful projects. I cannot also promise you that I will not think differently about aspects of it in the future. I might. All technology changes fast but Power BI changes faster than most. You might disagree with some of my opinions that I provide in the book. That is fine too. Take what you find useful. What I can tell you is this is how I have implemented a lot of projects, and very successfully.

Useful background knowledge

When you are reading this book, it will certainly help if you have some existing background with database management systems, and with building Power BI reports. It would be useful but not necessary for you to have some experience with tabular data models in Power BI, SQL Server Analysis Services, and/or Azure Analysis Services.

Structure of the book

There are twelve core chapters in the book. The content relates to a single-day course that I often teach on these topics.

In the **first** chapter, I will show you the end game. I want you to see what I am trying to achieve as an outcome. As part of that, I will show you some common scenarios that are often starting points for our projects. How I approach projects is not only driven by the technology. I often modify our approach based upon how comfortable the client already is with cloud-based technologies.

In the **second** chapter, I will tell you about the tools that I use.

In the **third** chapter, I will provide you an introduction to the identity and security concepts you need.

The **fourth** chapter discusses why you really need to create a separate data warehouse, and not just build your analytic work directly over existing relational databases and/or files.

I build databases using different schemas to provide structure. The DataModel schema is a core part of our designs. In the **fifth** chapter, I will show you how I structure that schema

In the **sixth** chapter, I will look at our Analytics schema. This is our connection point for Power BI, and for other tools like Microsoft Excel, or even SQL Server Reporting Services (for clients who are using that).

It is so important to manage your projects appropriately. In the **seventh** chapter, I will introduce Azure DevOps and to GitHub, to see how these might be part of your project management, and how they can be part of automated deployment.

In the **eighth** chapter, I will cover how I get data into the DataModel schema. This generally involves staging, loading, and transforming data.

There are two tools that I often use for controlling the transformation and processing of data. In the **ninth** chapter, I will describe how I use Azure Data Factory (ADF), and how I still might use SQL

Server Integration Services (SSIS) in some projects. I will show you how this all integrates with source code control and versioning.

The **tenth** chapter describes tabular data models and how I implement them in Azure Analysis Services, SQL Server Analysis Services, and/or Power BI Premium, depending upon the client's requirements. In this book, I do not have time for an extensive coverage of building tabular models, but I will describe the core work I do, and give you pointers to further information. The **eleventh** chapter rounds out the discussion on tabular models by covering how I implement tabular model processing and how I drive that from ADF. I will talk about row level security, how partitioning might be part of what is needed, and how I optimize the size of the deployed models.

The **twelfth** chapter finishes the discussion by noting a few aspects of how we then make data connections and start to build reports in Power BI.

There is quite a bit to cover; I hope you enjoy reading the book, and I hope it helps you to build better projects.

Chapter 1: Power BI Cloud Implementation Models

Overview

In this chapter, I want to show you what the end-game or result of our enterprise Power BI projects looks like. No two clients are identical, but there are groups of clients whose projects I manage in a particular way.

The key decider for us about how to implement a project, is the level of cloud maturity of the customer, and their existing source applications. I classify the clients into four categories:

- Cloud-native

- Cloud-friendly

- Cloud-conservative

- Cloud-unfriendly

Awesome image by Damir Kopezhanov

In this chapter, I will show you how I typically work with each of these types of clients.

Cloud-Native Clients

Characteristics

These clients are very comfortable with using cloud-based Software as a Service (SaaS) applications. They accept the idea that their data will reside in cloud-based storage. In most cases, they are already using cloud-based SaaS applications, and these will be the primary source systems for our analytic work.

Starting Point

These are our favorite clients. When I start working with them, the starting point often looks like this:

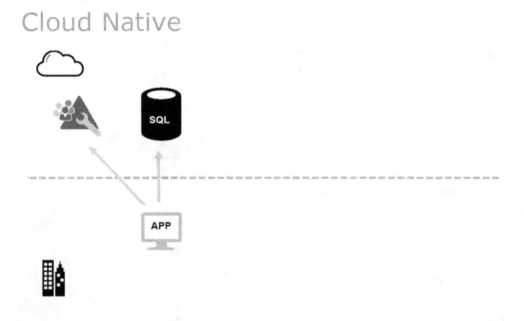

There will often be a cloud-based identity provider like Azure Active Directory but could be others. Ideally that identity provider will already be being used for all the cloud-based applications. Unfortunately, in many cases, there will be separate usernames and passwords for each of the cloud-based applications. The transactional data that I need to build analytics over, will already be in the cloud, and often in some form of SQL database.

Typical Implementation

For these clients, I will typically implement the following type of solution:

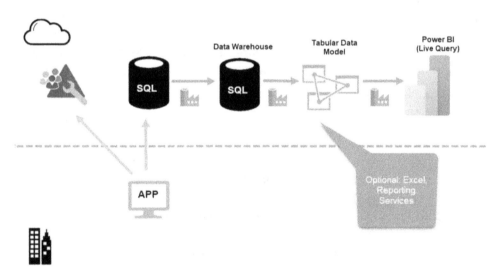

I create a data warehouse in Azure. Mostly I use Azure SQL Database. While I could potentially use Azure SQL Managed Instance or Azure Synapse Analytics, the costs associated with this are rarely justified for this part of our projects. Azure SQL Database is a great fit for this, and both scalable, and economic.

In that data warehouse, I will shape, cleanse, and perhaps version, the source data so that it is ready for use in analytics. I might also need to align the data coming from multiple source systems.

The outcome I am looking for is data that can be loaded directly into a tabular model.

For a tabular data model, I most commonly use Azure Analysis Services. I find it has an appropriate blend of capability and cost. The exception to this is if the client already has, or can justify the cost of, Premium Power BI licensing. Typically for us, that means clients who will have more than about 300 users of the final Power BI reports.

All the movement of data, and the processing of the tabular models is controlled by using Azure Data Factory (ADF).

An advantage of using Azure Analysis Services in this way, is that it is also a great point for connecting other tools like Microsoft Excel, or even SQL Server Reporting Services (SSRS) if the client wants to use that. Those connections also use the same row level security.

Note however that I do not recommend using Azure Analysis Services as the source of data for further transformation or ETL work. As an example, if the client also has tools like Tableau that need source data, I supply this from the data warehouse database that I have built, not from Azure Analysis Services.

Tools Used

For these projects, I would typically use these tools from the Microsoft stack:

- Azure Active Directory (AAD) for identity management

- Azure SQL Database (ASD) for creating a data warehouse

- Azure Analysis Services (AAD) or Power BI Premium (PBI-P) for the analytic (tabular) data model

- Azure Data Factory (ADF) for moving data and for orchestrating data movement and processing)

- Power BI (PBI) for reporting and visualization

- Azure DevOps (AzDO) for project management, source code control and versioning

Optionally:

- Microsoft Excel for ad-hoc queries over the analytic data model

- SQL Server Reporting Services (SSRS) or Power BI (PBI) for paginated reports

Azure SQL Database

You will notice that I prefer Azure SQL Database. It is the type of database that I try to use every time. You want to hand over day to day management of databases like this to Microsoft.

Today, for a database, you want a T-SQL end point to talk to, and you want to manage the database declaratively, not procedurally i.e., you want to say how big a database should be, how fast it should be, where it is located, if there is replica, and where that has located, and if the replica is readable, etc.

You do not want to be managing the low-level activities of how all that works. And you do not want to need to retain and train staff who know how to do those things.

I look at our own administrative databases. Years ago, I had them running on virtual machines, and there was constant work for me to keep them running and secure. From the point that I migrated them to Azure SQL Database, I have almost never thought about them again. They just work. That has what you want for your projects too.

Cloud-Friendly Clients

Characteristics

These clients are not already using cloud-based systems for their core work, but they are comfortable with the concept of using cloud-based Software as a Service (SaaS) applications. They accept the idea that a replica of some of their data that is required for analytics, will reside in cloud-based storage.

Starting Point

These are great clients to work with as they are much more open to the cloud-based approaches that I prefer. Typically, the starting point looks like this:

Cloud Friendly

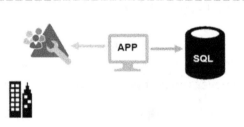

These clients typically have Active Directory (AD) implemented on-premises or in a private data center. They run applications on-premises and they have on-premises databases that will be the source of the analytics.

Typical Implementation

For these clients, I will typically implement the following type of solution:

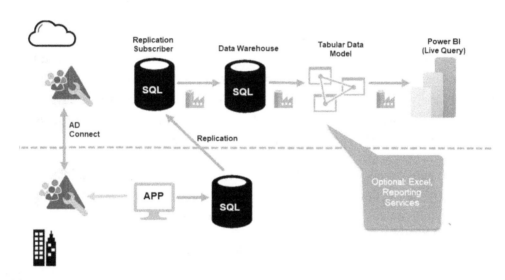

I start by implementing a hybrid identity. I am going to need to have an Azure AD based identity for Power BI anyway, so that has a good starting point. I create an Azure Active Directory (AAD) and set it up to sync with the on-premises AD via an application called AD Connect.

You can find more about hybrid identity here:

https://docs.microsoft.com/en-us/azure/active-directory/hybrid/cloud-governed-management-for-on-premises?WT.mc_id=DP-MVP-7914

You can find more about AD Connect here:

https://docs.microsoft.com/en-us/azure/active-directory/hybrid/whatis-azure-ad-connect?WT.mc_id=DP-MVP-7914

The next thing I try to do, is to get a copy of the source data into Azure with as low a latency as possible. If the source system is SQL Server, in many cases I can use Transactional Replication (TR) to constantly copy the data into Azure SQL Database. In recent years, the SQL Server team has given us the ability to create a TR subscriber in an Azure SQL Database. This can provide a simple, reliable option for providing a cloud-based replica of the data I am interested in.

Note: not all source applications will tolerate having Transactional Replication in place. If a third-party application is using the database, you will generally need to check with the authors of the application to see if this can be used. Otherwise, an alternate mechanism might be required.

Most of the rest of the project is then the same as with the cloud-native clients.

I create a data warehouse in Azure with another Azure SQL Database, and use Azure Analysis Services or Power BI Premium for analytic model, and Power BI for reporting and visualization.

As with the cloud-native projects, all the movement of data, and the processing of the tabular models is controlled by using Azure Data Factory (ADF).

Tools Used

For these projects, I would typically use these tools from the Microsoft stack:

- Azure Active Directory (AAD) and AD Connect for hybrid identity management

- Azure SQL Database (ASD) for both a replica database and for creating a data warehouse

- Azure Analysis Services (AAD) or Power BI Premium (PBI-P) for the analytic (tabular) data model

- Azure Data Factory (ADF) for moving data and for orchestrating data movement and processing)

- Power BI (PBI) for reporting and visualization

- Azure DevOps (AzDO) for project management, source code control and versioning

Optionally:

- Microsoft Excel for ad-hoc queries over the analytic data model

- SQL Server Reporting Services (SSRS) or Power BI (PBI) for paginated reports

Cloud-Conservative Clients

Characteristics

These clients are not already using cloud-based systems for their core work. They are willing to use Power BI in the cloud for visualizing data but are not prepared to store even their analytic data in the cloud.

Starting Point

These clients are much less open to the cloud-based approaches that I prefer. Typically, the starting point looks like this:

Cloud Conservative

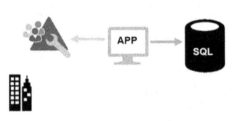

The starting point for these clients is often identical to the starting point for cloud-friendly clients. The difference is in their attitude to cloud-based systems. They typically have Active Directory (AD) implemented on-premises or in a private data center. They run applications on-premises and they have on-premises databases that will be the source of the analytics.

Typical Implementation

For these clients, I will typically implement the following type of solution:

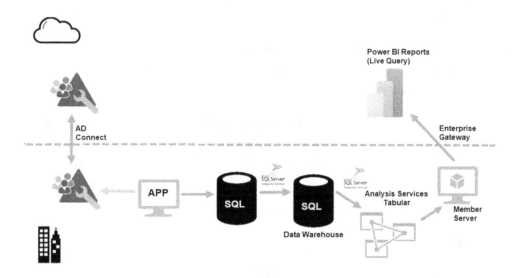

I start by implementing a hybrid identity. This is needed so that Power BI can be used for visualization. As with the cloud-friendly option, I create an Azure Active Directory (AAD) and set it up to sync with the on-premises AD via an application called AD Connect.

You can find more about hybrid identity here:

https://docs.microsoft.com/en-us/azure/active-directory/hybrid/cloud-governed-management-for-on-premises?WT.mc_id=DP-MVP-7914

You can find more about AD Connect here:

https://docs.microsoft.com/en-us/azure/active-directory/hybrid/whatis-azure-ad-connect?WT.mc_id=DP-MVP-7914

For these clients who have a focus on keeping data on-premises, I work with SQL Server and SQL Server Analysis Services.

I create a data warehouse as a database in SQL Server, often on the same server as they are using for their existing applications, but potentially a separate server. I then use SQL Server Analysis Services (SSAS) for the tabular data model.

I still use Power BI for the visualization, and I still use Live Query to the analytic model to be the source of data for Power BI. The difference is that because the SSAS server will be on-premises, Power BI will need to communicate with it through a Power BI Enterprise Gateway (EG). While the EG can in theory be installed on the SSAS server, that usually is not recommended, so it will be installed on another member server in the domain.

Enterprise Gateway

The Enterprise Gateway (EG) provides a secure way for Power BI to communicate queries to the SSAS server. Clients are often concerned that implementing a gateway will reduce security as it might require punching a hole in their inbound firewalls.

The great news is that has not how it works. The connections are initiated from within the local network, and they reach out to the Power BI service i.e., the connections used by the EG are all outbound connections. And at the point of connection, the EG exchanges certificates with the Power BI service for a secure authentication.

SQL Server Integration Services (SSIS)

Another difference from the cloud-friendly options is that I use SQL Server Integration Services (SSIS) instead of ADF for orchestrating the movement of data, for moving data, and for the processing of the SSAS tabular models.

SSIS a great tool for ETL (extract transform load) work or for ELT (extract load transform) work that is more common today. It is widely used and there is a great deal of online help available for working with it. Development in SSIS is done in SQL Server Data Tools (SSDT) in Visual Studio (VS), the same tooling used for developing tabular data models for SSAS.

If you need to learn about SSIS, I have an online course that should help:

https://sqldownunder.com/courses/sql-server-integration-services-for-developers-and-dbas

Tools Used

For these projects, I would typically use these tools from the Microsoft stack:

- Azure Active Directory (AAD) and AD Connect for hybrid identity management

- SQL Server databases

- SQL Server Analysis Services (SSAS)

- SQL Server Integration Services (SSIS)

- Power BI Enterprise Gateway (EG)

- Power BI (PBI) for reporting and visualization

- Azure DevOps (AzDO) for project management, source code control and versioning if the client is open to cloud-based source control, otherwise I use an on-premises Git repository and a separate project management tool. At the least, this will often I some form of Kanban board.

Optionally:

- Microsoft Excel for ad-hoc queries over the analytic data model

- SQL Server Reporting Services (SSRS) for paginated reports

Cloud-Unfriendly Clients

Characteristics

These clients are not into cloud-based solutions at all.

They want all their data to stay on-premises, and they want their analytic reporting to stay there too.

Starting Point

These clients are not open to the cloud-based approaches that I prefer. Typically, the starting point looks like this:

Cloud Unfriendly

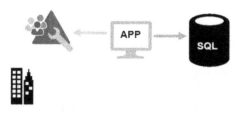

The starting point for these clients is often identical to the starting point for cloud-friendly and cloud-conservative clients. The difference again is in their attitude to cloud-based systems. They typically have Active Directory (AD) implemented on-premises or in a private data center. They run applications on-premises and they have on-premises databases that will be the source of the analytics.

Typical Implementation

For these clients, I will typically implement the following type of solution:

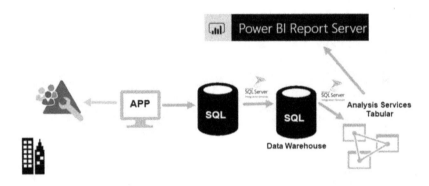

Cloud Unfriendly Implementation

For these customers, nothing will end up cloud-based.

I will continue to use their on-premises Active Directory for identity.

To keep data on-premises, I work with SQL Server and SQL Server Analysis Services.

I create a data warehouse as a database in SQL Server, often on the same server as they are using for their existing applications, but potentially a separate server. I then use SQL Server Analysis Services (SSAS) for the tabular data model.

36

For visualization and for paginated reports and subscriptions, I create Power BI reports and deploy them to an on-premises Power BI Report Server. This provides a far less capable outcome, but it is usually a step up from what they had before.

Again, I use SQL Server Integration Services (SSIS) instead of ADF for orchestrating the movement of data, for moving data, and for the processing of the SSAS tabular models.

Tools Used

For these projects, I would typically use these tools from the Microsoft stack:

- SQL Server databases

- SQL Server Analysis Services (SSAS)

- SQL Server Integration Services (SSIS)

- Power BI Report Server

- Azure DevOps (AzDO) for project management, source code control and versioning if the client is open to cloud-based source control, otherwise I use an on-premises Git repository and a separate project management tool. At the least, this will often I some form of Kanban board.

Optionally:

- Microsoft Excel for ad-hoc queries over the analytic data model

Chapter 2: Other Tools That I Often Use

Overview

In this chapter, I want to list several additional tools that I might use when working with projects. Not all projects will include each of these.

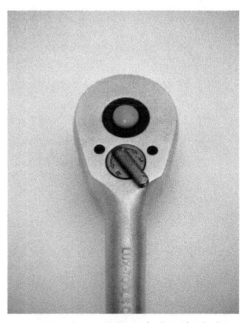

Awesome image by Everyday Basics

SQL Server Reporting Services

Given all the love shown today to cloud-based offerings, you could be forgiven for assuming that SQL Server Reporting Services (SSRS) would no longer be part of our projects, but that is not the case.

One of the mistakes that I see people making all the time is to be trying to use analytic tools to report on operational data. Analytic systems shine when they are producing strategic reports. The closer that you get to real-time reporting, the less likely it is that an analytic tool is the right option for reporting. It is rare that you will want to make a strategic decision based upon what has happened in the last few minutes in a transactional system.

If you need to produce a report on orders that should already have shipped, and the data needs to be accurate to the last few minutes, an analytic system and Power BI is unlikely to be an appropriate solution.

The more operational in nature your reports are, the more likely you will be better producing them in a tool like SSRS. show you what the result of our enterprise Power BI projects looks like. No two clients are identical, but there are groups of clients whose projects I manage in a particular way.

SSRS is still the best option today for paginated reports. Power BI Premium is improving but it still does not have the capabilities in this area that SSRS does. Even though it has been around a long time, there are areas where SSRS still shines.

I like the quote from Mark Twain where he said that "*The reports of my death are greatly exaggerated*". It is the same with SSRS.

SSRS Tooling

SSRS reports can be produced in a tool called SQL Server Report Builder but it people are more likely to produce them in SQL Server Data Tools (SSDT). If you are not familiar with SSDT, it is important to be aware of some changes in recent years. Originally this tool was called Business Intelligence Development Studio (BIDS) but in 2012 the name was changed to SSDT.

It was always an add-on (or extension) to Visual Studio (VS). If you happened to already have VS, it just installed itself as a new set of project templates. But you did not need to already have VS. If you did not, it installed the VS shell (also called the partner edition of VS). Up to VS 2017, there was a standalone installer for SSDT, and it was free.

With Visual Studio 2019 and later, this all changed. Instead of SSDT being shipped as a downloadable add-on, the SSRS designer became a separate Reporting Services Project extension to VS. It is now added and deleted through the VS menus. The same also applies to the Analysis Services Projects and Integration Services Projects.

Tabular Editor

Tabular Editor is an incredibly useful 3rd party tool written by Daniel Otykier. It is used to edit tabular data models. While you can already do that in SSDT, you can do it much easier in Tabular Editor.

I will mention more about this later in the book, but this is a nearly essential tool. It is a lightweight editor for tabular models. Up to version 2, Tabular Editor was free. Tabular Editor 3 is a paid product.

There are many actions that in the Analysis Services editor in VS that are just slow, particularly if I am trying to make changes to large data models. Tabular Editors lets you do many of these actions fast, working directly with the model rather than endlessly refreshing large amounts of data.

Another powerful aspect of Tabular Editor is its scripting engine. If you find yourself doing repetitive work on a tabular model, you can create a script to do that instead. Large numbers of changes can be applied to tabular models near instantly. For example, if I decided that every column with a name ending in Key (e.g., CustomerKey, ProductKey) should be hidden. I can just write a script to find and hide all of these at once. That can save me from a large amount of work in the editor.

A final key aspect of Tabular Editor that I will mention now is that it helps with letting more than one person edit a tabular model at the same time. Instead of everyone trying to edit a single **.bim** file, and then you having a nightmare trying to merge the changes, Tabular Editor lets you shred the file to a whole series of .json files that each represent part of the model. This works far better with source control and versioning. You can then later reassemble the .bim file if you want.

Tabular Editor also integrates with DAX Formatter to allow you to easily format your DAX code while editing.

This is a wonderful piece of technology. You will find it at https://tabulareditor.com it can also be added as an external tool directly into Power BI Desktop.

Vertipaq Analyzer

Another useful 3rd party tool is Vertipaq Analyzer. It is a free community tool contributed by the team at SQLBI (Marco Russo and Alberto Ferrari).

Vertipaq is the old internal name for the tabular data model. This utility is an Excel-based template that connects to a tabular data model and analyses the structures that it finds.

The tool is particularly useful when trying to optimize (mostly reduce) the size of tabular data models. It shows where all the space is being used, table by table, and column by column.

It can connect to tabular models in:

- SQL Server Analysis Services

- Azure Analysis Services

- Power BI Premium

- Power BI Desktop

It is also possible to analyze an Excel PowerPivot data model by importing it first into Power BI Desktop.

I find the easiest way to work with this tool now though, is to use it from within DAX Studio.

You will find the tool here: https://www.sqlbi.com/tools/vertipaq-analyzer/

DAX Studio

This is another essential 3rd party tool. And again, it is free. The prim
Darren Gosbell.

This is another tool that can be launched as an external tool directly from

If you are trying to write DAX code, this is the tool that you should wri
are still trying to learn to write DAX. The DAX editing experience in S
Projects) is quite poor.

It can connect to tabular models in:

- SQL Server Analysis Services

- Azure Analysis Services

- Power BI Premium

- Power BI Desktop

- SSDT Integrated Workspaces

- PowerPivot in Excel

As well as helping you write DAX queries, it lets you execute the queries, format the queries, and analyze the performance characteristics of the queries.

As I mentioned, this is an essential tool for your toolkit.

You will find this tool here: https://daxstudio.org

Azure Storage Explorer

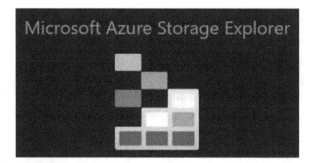

When you are working with enterprise Power BI projects, at some point you will need to work with storage accounts in Azure.

The tool that you want for doing that is another free tool from Microsoft called Azure Storage Explorer.

You can either connect to a storage account via your as your log on or by using primary or secondary storage account keys.

A bonus is that it now has an extension that lets you connect to Azure Data Factory (ADF) as well.

You will find this tool here: https://azure.microsoft.com/en-au/features/storage-explorer/

Chapter 3: Working with Identity

Overview

Many organizations that I work with have an extraordinary mess with identity. At one of my clients, I log onto an external Citrix system that handles external logins. From there, I open a virtual desktop. The virtual desktop in theory has the same credentials as the Citrix system, but they often get out of sync. From the virtual desktop, I then log into a virtual environment management system, using a different set of credentials. Once I have authenticated to that virtual environment management system, I then open a virtual lab environment using yet another set of credentials. Inside that environment, I might also need to work with different database credentials.

That is ridiculous.

Awesome image by Kyle Glenn

Identity Aims

The first aim for identity should be to have it as simple as possible, while retaining sufficient security. What I like to see though, is a single identity for the staff involved.

The second aim is that I want it to be a hybrid identity. The same identity should be usable in the cloud and within an on-premises domain.

My third aim is that the same identity should be able to be used with both in-house applications and with cloud-based Software as a Service (SaaS) applications. I do not want to have a proliferation of usernames and passwords. If my company wants to use ZenDesk for a helpdesk, and Jira for management, etc., I do not want to have separate credentials (usernames and passwords) for each SaaS application that the organization uses. Every time you have additional credentials for users, your overall security level goes down.

And my fourth aim is to have most of the security role-based, not user-based. By this, I mean that most times a user will get permission to use a resource because they are a member of a group (or role), not because someone game them permissions personally.

Once those aims are met, I then have a few optional ones I like to see.

If I am working with a partner organization and I need to access their resources, I would like to be using my normal company identity across in that other company, rather than an entirely different identity.

And finally, I might need to be able to provide access to my own company's systems for customers, clients, members, etc. I do not want applications within my company storing usernames and passwords for those external people.

It is often said that one of the biggest mistakes you can make in it projects, is trying to add security back in near the end of a project. It is important that you design and test your security mechanisms early on. In most organizations that I work with, a central it group will be responsible for identity and adding and changing security structures often needs layers of approvals. If that has the case in your organization, that has even more reason for working out what is needed early on, to avoid delaying your BI project.

Azure Active Directory

There are many tools in the market for managing identity. If you are using Power BI, you will already be using Azure Active Directory (AAD), so it is a great place to start.

One thing that has intrigued me in recent years, is that some organizations that I work with have purchased 3rd party identity management systems when they already have AAD. Almost every time, what I find is that they were unaware of what AAD can do i.e., they already had a product that did what was needed, and they then purchased another product to work with it. Before you go and purchase a 3rd party identity management system, make sure you have looked at what AAD can already do for you.

Azure AD Core Directory (AAD)

The core role that AAD plays is to provide a directory containing users, passwords, groups, devices, and more.

AAD makes it easy to integrate **Multi-Factor Authentication** (MFA). It is also possible for AAD to enable Single Sign On (SSO) from other identity providers (like Google, Facebook, etc.) but generally these would only be used for external people like customers, members, clients, patients, etc. For typical work within an organization, it is unlikely that these external identity providers could be used. Staff are unlikely to be allowed to log onto corporate systems using their Factbook identity, even if that has possible.

You can apply **branding** to login screens when using AAD, rather than just using the standard Azure logins. This can give your users more confidence that they are dealing with a login screen from your organization. The branding can apply an image to the overall background, and add logos, etc. to the login-related screens.

AAD also provides two other forms of access control.

Role Based Access Control (RBAC) is the way that you give users permission to use Azure resources. Users can be added to roles (a.k.a. groups), and those roles can be given permission to the resources.

Conditional Access allows you to control aspects of how users are connecting. For example, you can restrict the range of IP addresses that they are connecting from. You can also decide if MFA is required when connecting from within the organization, or if it is only needed when connecting from outside the organization.

Hybrid AD

When I start working with most organizations today, they have on-premises domain controllers, and they think of these as the primary authority for authentication. Over time, I believe that Azure Active Directory (AAD) will become the primary directory for most organizations. More and more applications and services will be cloud-based, and those will inevitably use AAD for authentication. There are already many thousands of cloud-based applications and services that will let you use AAD for authentication. For example, if you want to use ZenDesk for a helpdesk, or DropBox for storage, you can use your same organizational credentials for this. That has so far superior to having different credentials for each of the services that you use.

Today though, you will usually need to configure a hybrid approach. There will be an on-premises domain controller, and there will also be AAD. So, you will need a way to keep the two synchronized. The tool for doing that is called **AD Connect**.

There are three ways that AD Connect can function.

The first is that it can just do a **password hash sync**. AD Connect can copy your username and a hash of your password from your on-premises domain controller (DC) to AAD. When you log in to AAD, it can just check that the hash of your password matches. It does not ever need to have your actual password.

Some organizations would prefer that the hashed passwords do not leave the on-premises DC either. In that case, a second option can be used where AD Connect allows for a **pass-through** form of authentication. When a login attempt is received, AAD sends the username and a hash of the password that the user entered, to the on-premises DC, and that server performs the authentication and sends the result back to AAD. At no point does AAD ever need to store any password hashes.

48

The options above are easy to configure. The other option is that you can configure what is called **Federation**. This adds the AAD server into an existing Active Directory Federation Services (ADFS) configuration. Note, I have never needed to do this for any of the Power BI projects that I have worked on to-date.

When you are using AD Connect, you can also choose which objects are synchronized. You can control which users are synchronized, along with which groups and other objects.

Azure AD Business to Business (AAD B2B)

I have mentioned that I do mentoring or consulting work for client organizations. Identity is another challenge with this. For example, if I need to do work for Company A, they might create a login for me as g.low@companyA.com. Then when I do work for Company B, they will create another identity for me as Greg.Low@companyB.com and so on, and so on.

While each company might think they are doing a great job of security, when they do this, they are reducing security. I now need to juggle many sets of credentials. And every one of them will no doubt have different rules about how complex they need to be, and how often they need to be renewed.

Awesome image by Amy Hirschi

Nowadays, this is not a clever way to work. Instead, it would be better if I only ever logged into my own organization as greg@sqldownunder.com and each company I work for just enabled me to use that identity within their own systems. And that has precisely what **Azure AD B2B** does. It is about working with other businesses as partners.

Instead of creating me a new identity at each company, those companies can instead invite me into their directory in AAD. Then I can be added to roles and assigned permissions like other users within their own organization.

Note that when I get to a login screen, even though I am logging in with my own company's credentials, I see the branding from the inviting organization, not the branding from my own organization.

Azure AD Business to Consumer (AAD B2C)

A third mode that AAD can operate in is called B2C (or Business to Consumer).

As well as your own staff (AAD), partner organizations' staff (AAD B2B), most organizations have a need to store details of the people that they deal with as part of their operations. For example, a medical clinic will have patients, a superannuation company (or retirement fund) will have members, a sales organization will have customers, and so on.

If these consumers need to be able to log onto your systems, their authentication details will need to be stored somewhere. The traditional older approach for this was for your own systems to store usernames and password hashes. (Sadly, I still even see corporate systems storing actual passwords).

Awesome image by Timon Studler

Today, you should not be doing this! Every time you consider rolling your own authentication system, you need to stop and remind yourself that doing so is a poor idea. Getting this type of system correct and bug-free is tough. Look at the issues with authentication that Microsoft, Google, and others have. And they have thousands of staff members trying to get it right, let alone the amount of work they do to detect and avoid various types of attack. Just do not do this.

Instead, consider outsourcing the authentication of your consumers to a tool like AAD B2C. It is designed to do this. With AAD B2C, your consumers can use any email address or username as an identity, and you can also easily enable standard social identity providers like Facebook, LinkedIn, etc.

This can be particularly useful if you are considering Power BI Embedded as part of your solution.

AAD and Azure Databases

If you are working with databases in Azure, you can also integrate with Azure AD based identities.

Azure SQL

Azure SQL Database and Azure SQL Managed Instance can have an AAD administrator assigned. For this, I typically assign an AAD group as the administrator, and separately add AAD users to that group, so they are all capable of managing the databases.

You can also create users in Azure SQL Database that are based upon AAD identities. I commonly do this when I need a service like Azure Data Factory (ADF) to connect to the database.

One trick to be aware of is that you can only add users based upon AAD identities, while you yourself are connected using an AAD based admin identity. You cannot add these while logged on as a SQL Server authenticated login or user.

Azure Analysis Services

You can also configure Azure Analysis Services (AAS) with AAD identities as both users and administrators.

AAD identities are also the basis of row level security (RLS) in AAS.

Service Principals

There is a special type of AAD based identity known as a Service Principal (SP). Originally, the most common use for service principals was to provide a way for an application to authenticate to Azure AD, rather than the user who was running the application.

A service principal was created by:

- Creating an Application in Azure AD

- Noting the ApplicationID that was created, and the TenantID (i.e., the ID of the entire Azure tenant or domain)

- Creating a Secret for the Application and noting the Secret.

When you create a secret in the portal, you are only shown the secret just after you create it. It is important to copy it at that point as you cannot find it in the portal again later.

When an application needs to authenticate, it passes the ApplicationID, the TenantID, and the Client Secret to AAD. If the combination is valid, a login token is returned.

Managed Service Identities

A special type of service principal is called a Managed Service Identity (MSI). These are used when services need to authenticate to resources. For example, I might be using Azure Data Factory (ADF) to move data around, and it needs to connect to an Azure SQL Database.

The mistake that I see many people make, is that they create a SQL login for this situation. Do not do that. Instead, the instance of ADF has its own identity. That has the managed service identity. It is a special identity managed by Azure and you can assign permissions to it, just like another other user identity. You can then create a user in Azure SQL Database for the ADF MSI and grant it permissions. The same identity can be used to connect to other services that ADF might need, like Azure Key Vault for storing secrets.

Note though, that not all Azure services have MSIs available. One current glaring omission is that Azure Analysis Services (AAS) and Power BI do not currently offer MSIs. You can connect to AAS using an MSI, but AAS does not have an MSI that could be used, for example, when AAS needs to connect to a database. I do hope Microsoft rectifies this as soon as possible.

Chapter 4: Do you need a Data Warehouse?

Overview

I often watch webinars where the presenter connects Power BI directly to a source transactional database to start building analytics. If it is possible to do this, you then need to ask yourself if you still need to build a data warehouse.

Betteridge's law says that if you see one of these types of questions on the Internet, the answer is always **NO**.

But contrary to that, if you want the short story from this chapter, the answer is **YES**.

The quality of the analytics that you build is almost entirely dependent upon the quality of the data that you build it upon. I prefer to build a data warehouse in almost every project, and to attach the analytics to that.

Awesome image by Simone Secci

I see tools that advertise how you can just create your analytics directly over the source relational databases and all will be good. That sounds great in theory, but the outcomes that I see from doing this are dreadful. The analytics are usually poor, and you are likely to also create performance problems, either in the analytics, or in the source system, or in both.

The issues that I see with analytics directly over relational systems mostly fall into these categories:

- Poor transformation code

- Lack of code re-use

- Inconsistent outcomes

- Performance issues

What is needed is:

- A clean model for building analytics

- A model focused on analytics, not focused on relational workloads

- Directly human readable/presentable output

- Consistent data cleansing and validation

And you might also need:

- To align data from multiple source systems

- To be able to version data

- To have a way to provide for longer-term storage and reporting

A separate data warehouse is still the best place to achieve these aims. Let us look at a few core aspects.

Cleansing Data

There are many aspects to cleansing data but let me provide you with some simple examples of the types of cleansing that is needed.

Appropriate Naming

Source transactional database systems are notorious for containing poorly named objects. Here is an example of some table names from one system:

ST	Students
DF	Families
SF	Staff
SXAB	Half Day Attendances
SXABCONV	Converted Student Half-Day Absences
UM	Addresses
KCL	Languages
KGT	Countries
SCI	School Information
SKGS	All Schools

The left-hand column is the names of the tables in the database. The right-hand column is an attempt at determining what data the tables hold.

Some systems are cryptic. Others are intentionally opaque.

Consistency

For your analytic work to look great, the incoming data must be consistent.

As a simple example, you do not want a customer with a name of **COMPANY A LTD** and another customer with a name of **Company B Ltd**.

You often need to clean up casing, etc. from data values. It could be that the source system users are just haphazard or lazy in how they enter data, or it could be that you are needing to combine data from multiple systems, and the data in each system has been created in a different way.

There is also a consistency-related need in categorizing data. For example, if you have a list of sports like:

- Soccer

- Tennis

- Volleyball

- Basketball

- Football

And in your area, both Football and Soccer mean the same thing, the outcome of your analytics can be inappropriately skewed.

Schema Design

In a data warehouse, I want to have simple relationships between tables. In most cases, this will be based upon a single integer value (int or bigint).

Source systems will often have much wider keys.

```
CREATE CLUSTERED INDEX [Impressions] ON [d
(
    [ImpressionDay] ASC,
    [AdvertiserID] ASC,
    [BannerID] ASC,
    [CampaignID] ASC,
    [ZoneID] ASC,
    [UserID] ASC,
    [CountryCode] ASC,
    [RegionCode] ASC,
    [BrowserID] ASC,
    [PlatformID] ASC,
    [MetroCode] ASC,
    [LanguageID] ASC,
    [DemographicID1] ASC,
    [DemographicID2] ASC,
    [DemographicID3] ASC,
    [DemographicID4] ASC
) WITH (PAD_INDEX = OFF, STATISTICS_NORECC
GO
```

When I first saw the code in figure above, I thought I was looking at a table design. In fact, I was looking at the design of a clustered index on the table, and that was being used as a key to lookup values in the table.

Even in the source system, this was completely inappropriate. But I certainly do not want designs like this leaking into my analytics.

Data Types

Many source systems will have inappropriate data types.

For example, ever since SQL Server 2005 we were supposed to stop using the text, ntext, and image data types, yet I see them in systems all the time. I do not want them in the databases that I am working on. In fact, I also do not want other data types like smalldatetime, money, smallmoney.

Apart from data types that I would rather not use, there is also inappropriate use of data types in the source systems. For a value that is essentially Boolean (i.e., it is true of false), I do not want char(1) or varchar(1) columns holding 'Y' or 'N'. I want a bit data type column.

Invalid Data

If you are presenting analytics with data that is clearly wrong, it is easy to undo all the good work that you did with laying out great reports and visuals.

I am surprised how often I see mistakes in weather-related sites. I chose these issues, not because I work with weather sites, but because they demonstrate common mistakes. Here is a screenshot from a weather forecast site:

Wayne Hart's 5-day forecast

Today	Tonight	Saturday	Sunday	Monday	Tuesday
Sun & Clouds, Warmer	Partly Cloudy	Partly Cloudy	Partly Sunny, Breezy & Cooler	Sun & Clouds	Partly Cloudy, Warmer
52°	33°	53° 34°	48° 33°	48° 3320°	54° 37°

Watch NEWS 25 for weather changes throughout the day

It all looks quite good until you look at the temperature for Monday night. Clearly something went very wrong there. My best guess is that somehow a hexadecimal 20 (i.e., a space character) was appended to the end of the temperature. Either way, the data looks silly.

Years ago, I used to work with an operating system called Oasis. It was later rebranded to Theos. I recently visited their website to see if they still existed and found this.

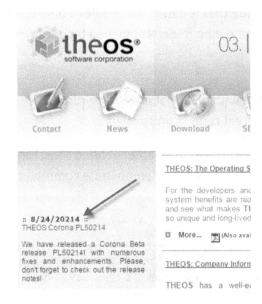

It is surprising that the formatting function that they had used for the date even allowed the year 20214. But that has certainly not when that happened.

Here is a local weather forecast.

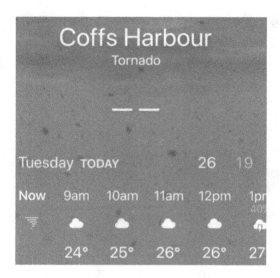

The simple truth here, is that Coffs Harbour does not ever have tornados. I cannot imagine what went wrong in this system, but that has so far from reality as to be laughable to a user seeing it.

Missing Data

Missing data is a particular challenge.

Some systems happily return missing data as blanks, but others make the mistake of using what I call **magic values**. These are values that are stored just like real values but are intended to mean something different to their stored values.

Here is another weather site:

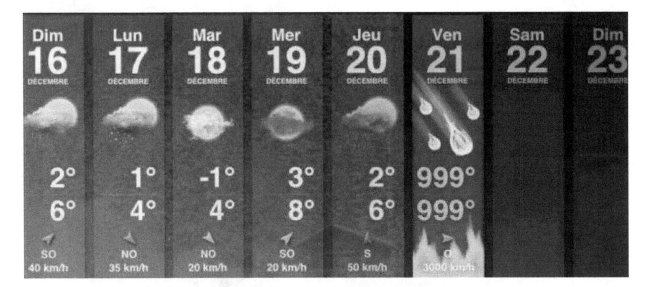

My best guess on this one is that when data was not present, instead of a NULL value being returned, the system was configured to return 999. The problem is that the developer working on the user interface did not know that could occur and has applied a rule to show the value.

If I have data that has missing, I want it to be NULL.

Unrealistic Data

Other times, you will find data that is present but does not reflect reality.

I commonly find this with columns like postal codes. Perhaps the system insisted that a postal code was provided (i.e., it was a mandatory column) but no data was available, so the value 9999 was inserted in every row, or even just in rows that did not have data.

Here is yet another weather site:

In this case, there is data, but it is clearly not valid data.

Rounding Issues

I regularly work with financial systems. Applying appropriate rounding rules is critical.

Inappropriate rounding can make your analytics fail.

I particularly liked this competition site:

You're in today's draw - Good Luck!

The draw will take place shortly after midnight.
You could be the lucky winner of a

XBOX 360 & Game!

Currently there are 132 players in today's draw.
You have a 0% chance of winning!

CONTINUE >

Now to the nearest integer, your chance of winning the competition probably is zero percent. My guess is that when the developer was working on this screen, there were only 10 or 20 players in the draw, and he or she always saw a valid looking value.

The key point is that no matter how much work you do on the visuals and presentation, your entire work can be undone by inappropriate data values.

Where to Cleanse Data

I certainly do not want to be doing this type of cleansing within an analytic tool. It is far easier to manipulate large amounts of data in a database. SQL based processes usually far outperform the alternatives.

A bonus of cleaning the data in a data warehouse, is that the cleansed data is then available for other tools that need it (e.g., perhaps SQL Server Reporting Services) not just the main analytic tool.

Databases also have a much stronger source control and versioning story than most analytic tools today.

Aligning Data from Multiple Systems

Another challenge arises when you need to combine and align data from multiple source systems. The different systems will often represent the same data in different ways. For example, an employee might be 12456 in a human resources or payroll system, yet the same employee might be FRED132 in the sales order system. This data will need to be aligned before it can be used sensibly.

Mapping and Reference Tables

As part of aligning data from different systems, you might need a set of mapping tables that convert values from one system to another.

For all data ingestion, even for a single table, you might also need a set of reference tables. A good example might be a table of all countries in the world.

Where to Align or Map Data

Once again, a data warehouse is a great place to perform aligning and mapping of data. The mapping and reference tables will need to live somewhere, and the data warehouse is an appropriate place.

Again, the performance of this will be better in SQL, and the integration with source control and versioning will be stronger.

Data Versioning

In some systems, you will need to represent changes in data over time.

The most common example of this for those using Kimball dimensional data models is the concept of slowly-changing dimensions.

As a simple example, imagine that you have a sales system and customers are allocated into sales territories. If today you decide to move customers around between sales territories, the issue is with what happens when you look at last year's data.

Does all the old data now appear categorized into the new sales territories? Or does the old data still appear in the same sales territories that it would have back when it was created?

It is important to understand that both scenarios might make sense to the business. They might want to see the old data in the new sales territories, or they might want to still see it as it was, or, perhaps, even both.

Where Should You Version Data?

No surprise at this point that I think a data warehouse is a great place to perform versioning of data. In most analytic tools, this is especially difficult. Most are not great at creating multiple rows from single rows of incoming data and versioning across time.

The performance of this will be better in SQL, and the integration with source control and versioning will again be stronger.

Maintaining Historical Data

I have recently been mentoring staff at a timber mill. They generate a large amount of data about every board they produce, and they produce a lot of boards.

The volume of data will not fit in common analytic models, but I do not want to lose the data. In fact, I still want to be able to query individual board data from years ago.

My analytic model is going to have board level data back for about three months and will hold aggregate data for the older boards.

Where to Maintain Historical Data

A database is the logical place to hold large amounts of historical data, at least if I ever want to be able to query it again.

In some data warehouse designs, I see the source data stored as files for historical data, and then if a query ever needs to be run, it is loaded again from those files.

Given the size of databases today, it is easy to store very large amounts of data, directly in the database. Even a small Azure SQL Database like an S0 tier can hold up to 250GB of data.

The data is already cleansed so it immediately usable by a variety of tools. You could run Direct Query reports from Power BI connected to the data, without importing any of it into a tabular model.

By holding the data in a data warehouse, it is ready for use when needed, but the analytic models are not bloated from holding it unnecessarily.

What I do: Data Warehouse

I try to leave the source systems unchanged where I can. As described, they are usually not ready for use with analytics anyway.

I then create a database to be used as a data warehouse.

Cloud-Native and Cloud-Friendly Customers

For all except cloud-native and cloud-friendly customers, I create an Azure SQL Database. I could use an Azure SQL Managed Instance or SQL Server in an Azure Virtual Machine, but I have a strong preference for an Azure SQL Database.

I start by provisioning an Azure SQL Server. It is not like an on-premises SQL Server and is more like a logical endpoint. On that server, I do the following:

- Configure a SQL authenticated administrator

- Configure the server's firewall (Often this will include a list of permitted IP addresses that users can connect from)

- Create an Azure Active Directory (AAD) group for the administrators of the server

- Configure the new group as the AAD Administrator for the Azure SQL Server.

I then provision an Azure SQL Database attached to that server. I do the following:

- Create a database project in source control (discussed later in the book)

- Add a database master key (to allow us to store credentials later when needed)

- Add our standard schemas

- Add our SDU Tools (https://sdutools.sqldownunder.com) to make it easier to build the data warehouse code

- Import the deployed database into the database project in source control, as a starting point.

69

Cloud-Conservative and Cloud-Unfriendly Customers

For these customers, I will not be holding their data in the cloud.

Instead, I will provision a SQL Server database on an existing on-premises SQL Server system. I will then:

- Create a database project in source control (discussed later in the book)

- Add a database master key (to allow us to store credentials later when needed)

- Add our standard schemas

- Add our SDU Tools (https://sdutools.sqldownunder.com) to make it easier to build the data warehouse code

- Import the deployed database into the database project in source control, as a starting point.

Then I am ready to start creating the main code in the data warehouse. I will be starting by looking at our DataModel schema.

Chapter 5: Implementing the DataModel Schema

Overview

The heart of the data warehouses that I create is the DataModel schema. It holds the cleansed and transformed data that can be used in a variety of ways.

It often will hold more data, and for a longer time, than is required for analytics.

Awesome image by Sam Moqadam

Database Schemas

When you are working with SQL Server, it is important to understand the use of schemas. Far too many databases today make no use of schemas.

Object Schemas

Look at the table creation code below:

```
CREATE TABLE Customers
(
        CustomerID int IDENTITY(1, 1) PRIMARY KEY,
        CustomerName varchar(100) NOT NULL

);
```

There are several things that I would do differently when writing a table creation script, but I wanted to just focus on the name of the table. By default, if you execute the code above, it will create a table named **Customers** but, in a schema, called **dbo**. The table's name would be **dbo.Customers**.

However, that assumes that your default schema was still dbo. If instead, your login had a default schema of **Sales**, the same code would create a table named **Customers** in the **Sales** schema instead. The table's name would be **Sales.Customers**.

This is one of the reasons why you should always prefix your table names with the required schema name, to make sure you get the outcome that you need. Another reason is related to performance and the way that code is cached in SQL Server.

You will find that the core SQL Server documentation always recommends using two-part names (schema and then object name) for all objects. That includes tables, function, stored procedures, and more.

Schemas for Grouping

Other database engines use schemas differently, but in SQL Server a schema is really two things:

- Grouping related objects
- Providing a security boundary for objects

Grouping objects is important. In the same way that you do not have all the files on your computer's hard drive in a single folder, you do not want to have all the tables and other objects in SQL Server in a single schema. Schemas can work just like folders.

I often see people using prefixes at the start of table names when they are trying to group objects. Look at this example from the Microsoft AdventureWorksDW database:

```
⊞ ▦ dbo.DimEmployee
⊞ ▦ dbo.DimGeography
⊞ ▦ dbo.DimOrganization
⊞ ▦ dbo.DimProduct
⊞ ▦ dbo.DimProductCategory
⊞ ▦ dbo.DimProductSubcategory
⊞ ▦ dbo.DimPromotion
⊞ ▦ dbo.DimReseller
⊞ ▦ dbo.DimSalesReason
⊞ ▦ dbo.DimSalesTerritory
⊞ ▦ dbo.DimScenario
⊞ ▦ dbo.FactAdditionalInternationalProductDescription
⊞ ▦ dbo.FactCallCenter
⊞ ▦ dbo.FactCurrencyRate
⊞ ▦ dbo.FactFinance
⊞ ▦ dbo.FactInternetSales
⊞ ▦ dbo.FactInternetSalesReason
⊞ ▦ dbo.FactResellerSales
```

Notice that all the tables are in the dbo schema, and these tables have a prefix of either Dim or Fact. This is a common pattern that you will find in many BI systems even today. The problem is that this structure first appeared before SQL Server 2005 when schemas were added. Too many people have just continued using it, even though we now have schemas.

When I see a list of tables that all have the same prefix, I know that the author is trying to group the tables together.

Instead of a set of tables like dbo.DimEmployee, dbo.DimProduct, etc. the structure would be far better if there was a Dimension schema (that has what the Dim was short for), and the tables were in that schema without prefixes e.g. Dimension.Employee and Dimension.Product, etc.

Schemas for Security

It is important to control who has access to your databases, and to limit that access to only what is required.

A common mistake in database and application design is to have applications connect to the database as a database owner (i.e., a member of the dbo role). This is never a good idea. If anyone gains control of your application (and that happens far more often than you might be aware of), they can then do anything at all that they want with your database.

Some developers use slightly more restrictive fixed database roles. They assign the user that an application connects with, to a role like db_datareader and/or db_datawriter. Even though it is surprisingly common as well, this is again not a good idea. Every time you grant someone access to a fixed role, you are granting them a bucket of permissions that often includes far more permissions than they need.

What you should do instead, is to create a role that has just the required permissions and grant membership of that role instead.

By far the easiest way to do this is to use schemas to implement the security. You can assign permissions to users and groups at the schema level, without having to assign permissions to all the objects in the schema.

In our data warehouses, I put all the objects that should be accessed by analytic applications into a schema called Analytics. Then all that I grant to the external application is the permission to SELECT and EXECUTE on the Analytics schema.

Our Analytics schema only ever has views, functions, and stored procedures that I want analytic tools to be able to use. This means that a cloud-based analytic tool that connects this way, will never be able to do more than SELECT and/or EXECUTE the objects in the Analytics schema.

I will discuss the Analytics schema later in the book.

DataModel Schema in the Data Warehouse Structure

When I structure these projects, I separate all our logic into a series of schemas. The overall flow of the data is as follows:

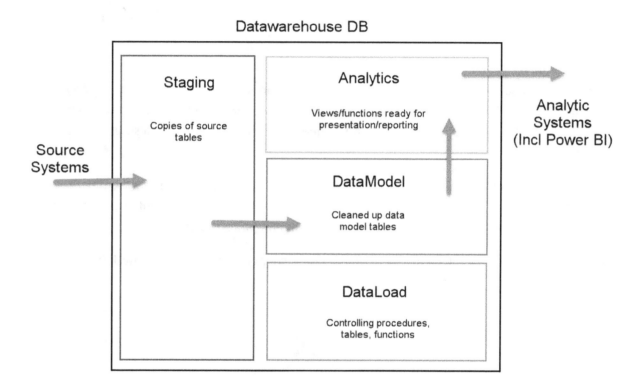

Source system data is usually from another database, or it might be from a series of files. No matter where it comes from, I start by bringing the data into a **Staging** schema.

The data in the Staging schema is cleansed and transformed and the outcome of that process is the **DataModel** schema. The data in the DataModel schema is ready to be consumed, and ready to be stored longer term if that is required.

The **Analytics** schema is a series of views (and occasionally functions) that are ready to be consumed by analytic tools like Analysis Services or Power BI. Apart from keys, the names are human readable and presentable, without the need for further renaming. I also use this schema as a security boundary.

The process of orchestrating the moving and cleansing of data is performed by the objects in the **DataLoad** schema. They are usually stored procedures and functions but might also involve tables for meta-data driven automation, or for reference and mapping tables.

I will look at the other schemas later, but in this chapter, you will see how I structure the DataModel schema.

DataModel Schema Design Goals

For the DataModel schema, I have the following goals:

- Provide a clean model for building analytics

- Use a design that is focused on analytics, not on transactional or highly-normalized relational work

- Use very clean and consistent naming

- Use consistent data types

- Use consistent abbreviations

- Validate data as required

I might also need to do the following:

- Combine data from multiple systems

- Version the data as it changes over time

Here is an example of the DataModel schema:

```
⊞ ▦ DataModel.CustomerBackorders
⊞ ▦ DataModel.CustomerInvoiceLines
⊞ ▦ DataModel.CustomerInvoices
⊞ ▦ DataModel.CustomerOrderLines
⊞ ▦ DataModel.CustomerOrders
⊞ ▦ DataModel.Customers
⊟ ▦ DataModel.CustomerSpecialPrices
   ⊟ ▦ Columns
      ⊷ CustomerSpecialPriceKey (PK, int, not null)
      ▤ CustomerKey (int, not null)
      ▤ StockItemKey (int, not null)
      ▤ DiscountPercentage (decimal(18,3), not null)
      ▤ DiscountAmount (decimal(18,2), not null)
      ▤ EstablishedDate (date, not null)
      ▤ CostAtTime (decimal(18,2), not null)
      ▤ IsPriceOverride (bit, not null)
      ▤ PromotionStartDate (date, not null)
      ▤ PromotionEndDate (date, not null)
```

Design Rules

Table Structures

The tables that I design will be focused on the requirements of the analytics. It is important to understand that it would be quite rare for the tables in the DataModel schema to map directly to the tables from the incoming source systems.

A good example is that I might flatten out source tables. A combination of an InvoiceHeader and InvoiceDetail table is likely to just become a single DataModel.Invoices table.

I avoid excessive normalization in these tables and focus more on providing simple analytics for the end user. Normalization is still a great goal in transactional databases but in analytic data warehouses, duplication of some data might be desirable.

Look at the two tables below:

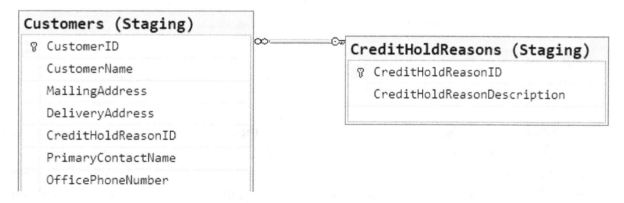

The source system has a table named Customers that has a column CreditHoldReasonID that is a reference to the CreditHoldReasons table. In that table, you can find the CreditHoldReasonDescription.

It is very likely that I would change the tables in the DataModel in this way:

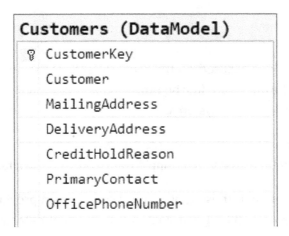

Instead of having the two normalized tables, I would take the column CreditHoldReasonDescription and add it directly to the Customers table. The column CreditHoldReasonID will not appear in the DataModel layer at all.

Note also that I tend to avoid columns that end in "Name" or "Description". In analytics, ProductName is usually better as just Product. Similarly, CreditHoldReasonDescription is better just as CreditHoldReason.

Low cardinality tables like this are better collapsed into the referencing tables, rather than adding to the complexity of the final model. In transactional systems, these types of codes might have been used to save space but with the columnstore storage provided by the tabular data model engine in Analysis Service and Power BI, the duplication of the values does not lead to additional storage requirements.

The result is that I usually have less tables in the DataModel schema than in the source, and they are usually simpler tables.

Appropriate Naming

Consistent naming is important in any analytic project.

Here are some general rules that I apply to the DataModel table and column naming:

- While the underlying structure of the design for the DataModel tables will lend itself to a star schema, I no longer use Dim (or Dimension) and Fact as part of our table names.

- I use plural table names in this schema. The one exception to this is if there is a table that will only ever hold a single row. It is important to focus on what each row in the table represents. I start with a name for a single row and then form the plural of that. So, for example, I could have a table called Customers, but I would not ever have a table called CustomerList or CustomerLedger. Those names do not have any obvious singular version. Better to first establish the name of what an individual row represents i.e., Customer and then find the plural of that i.e., Customers.

- I use PascalCased table and column names e.g., CustomerName and PromotionStartDate.

- For boolean (or true/false) columns, the names of the columns will have an action verb as a prefix e.g., IsValid or HasEnded. Typical action verbs are Is, Are, Has, Was, etc. but other values are fine. They just need to naturally lead to a true or false conclusion.

- I avoid any negative logic in the naming. Instead of a column named IsInvalid, I create the column IsValid and store the opposite of the value that would have gone into an IsInvalid column. Users understand positive Boolean values much better.

- I avoid abbreviations that are not necessary, but some use of abbreviations is acceptable if the abbreviations are very well understood in the client organization. For example, Max, Min, Avg might be acceptable, but I would be unlikely to use "Tot" and would instead write Total.

- If the value contains a date, my column name will end with Date e.g., LastSalesDate. Note however, that a column ending in Date would never have both a date and time stored. I would say LastSalesDateTime for that.

- If a value contains a time, my column name will end with Time e.g., LastSalesTime.

- If a column name ends with Name or Description, I generally create it without those suffixes i.e., CustomerName becomes Customer and ProductDescription becomes Product.

Data Types

SQL Server has many data types. I do not use them all.

In the DataModel schema, I usually restrict the list of data types to:

- int

- bigint

- bit

- decimal

- varchar

- nvarchar

- date

- time

- datetime (or datetime2)

I am very cautious about using datetime (or datetime2) columns in these models. If you load them into tabular analytic models, they compress very poorly. Even though I might have them present in the DataModel tables, I will consider carefully whether they need to also go into the analytic models. Date values are often all that is needed in analytics. If time is required, I will consider loading date and time values separately to improve the size of the analytic models.

I rarely use the following data types but, in some projects, they might be required:

- time
- float
- binary

The following data types are deprecated, and I do not use them:

- text
- ntext
- image

While the following data types are not deprecated, I avoid them:

- tinyint
- smallint
- smallmoney
- money
- xml
- real
- char
- nchar
- hierarchyid

Spatial data types (geography and geometry) are a potential exception to the rules above. For most analytic tools like Power BI, I am better storing locations of points as latitude and longitude as decimal values. Some reporting systems though can work with the spatial types, and I might store them in addition to the latitude and longitude (or X and Y) values. If I do that, those values will not be loaded into the tabular data models.

Spatial values that are not single point locations e.g., rectangles, are unlikely to be of use in my analytic models.

To check the consistency of the allocated data types, I will often use one of our free SDU Tools to check the values that I have used. The tool is called **ListMismatchedDataTypes**. It looks through a database and checks for columns that have the same name but are defined differently. For example, if there is a PhoneNumber column in one table defined as nvarchar(20) and in another table as nvarchar(15), or even defined with a different data type.

I will mention more about SDU Tools later in the book, but you can see a video of this tool in use here: https://youtu.be/i6mmzhu4T9g.

Table Keys and Relationships

Like a Kimball dimensional model, every table in the DataModel schema will have a Key column. This is either int or bigint. Generally, it is int in what you might consider "dimensions", and bigint in what you might consider "facts".

I name the table's key as the singular form of the table name followed by Key. The DataModel.Customers table will have a CustomerKey column. The DataModel.CustomerSpecialPrices table will have a CustomerSpecialPriceKey column.

All relationships between the tables are based on keys and only involve single columns.

Both surrogate and natural keys are used, depending upon the situation.

If I need to load details of sticks being produced by a sawmill, and if each stick already has a unique bigint identifier, I will use that natural value for the StickKey.

In all other situations, I will generate a surrogate key. To auto-generate keys, I use sequences rather than IDENTITY columns. Sequences were introduced in SQL Server 2005 and have many advantages over IDENTITY columns. There are others, but here are some of the reasons that I prefer them:

- Sequences are easier to manipulate with T-SQL and do not require DBCC commands, etc. when adjusting them.

- A single sequence can be used across multiple tables. (That has less useful in this DataModel layer but important elsewhere).

- You can easily adjust the caching of sequences. This can help with performance tuning.

- Sequences work across linked servers as expected. (For example, SET IDENTITY INSERT ON does not work across linked servers when you are trying to move data with IDENTITY columns).

I create the sequences in the same schema as the table, and the sequences have the same name as the key column as per the following example:

```
CREATE TABLE DataModel.Customers
(
    CustomerKey int
        CONSTRAINT PK_DataModel_Customers PRIMARY KEY
        CONSTRAINT DF_DataModel_Customers_CustomerKey
            DEFAULT (NEXT VALUE FOR DataModel.CustomerKey),
    CustomerID int NOT NULL,
    Customer varchar(50),
    MailingAddress varchar(max),
```

Note also that I always name the primary key constraints of tables. If you do not do this, the system will assign its own names. That leads to poor outcomes, particularly with database comparison tools as each time the script is executed, a different name will be generated. It also makes it easier to change details about a constraint (or remove it) when you already know its name.

For primary keys, I use a naming scheme of PK_SchemaName_TableName.

I also name default values, for similar reasons. As an example, if you need to drop a column, you first need to drop any default constraint on the column. It helps to know what the name of the default constraint is.

For defaults, I use a naming scheme of DF_SchemaName_TableName_ColumnName.

Business keys are stored as table columns. For numeric values, I generally use a name with an ID or Number suffix. For alphabetic values, I generally use a name with Code as the suffix. These business keys are almost always indexed.

Versioning Table Rows

In his books on dimensional modeling, Ralph Kimball talked about Slowly Changing Dimensions (SCDs). These were dimensions (like Customers, Categories, Products, etc.) that were used to categorize facts (like Invoices, Payments, etc.) and changed slowly over time.

For example, the color of a product might change occasionally.

As another example, consider a company that allocates their customers into sales territories. If they change which customers are in which sales territories today, what happens when they look at last year's sales data, broken down by sales territory? Is all the old data now in the new territories? Or does the data still look the same as it used to?

There is no one right answer for this. Both business cases are possible. You need to decide how this should affect your analytics.

If you are happy to just always see the latest version of old data, then no special action is needed. But if you want to have both the old allocations as well as the new ones, you need to version your data.

The standard approach for doing that is to add additional rows with the same business keys, but with new surrogate keys.

If I have a Customer row with a CustomerKey of 296, and a CustomerID of 12 (i.e., the business key or the ID in the source system), when a change occurs, I create a new Customer row. It will have a CustomerKey (a new value, let us say 1923), and the same CustomerID of 12. Old facts will still be linked to the original row, and new facts will be linked to the new version of the customer.

By doing this, you can either look at customer details across all of time (by using the CustomeriD) or details of when the customer had different values (by using the CustomerKey).

Additional Columns

When I implement SCDs as above, I will usually add two additional columns to the table:

- StartDateTime (or even just StartDate if possible)

- EndDateTime (or even just EndDate if possible)

The date columns will be used to indicate the period during which the version of the row is valid.

There are two ways to handle the EndDateTime (or EndDate) values. For the "current" row, there really is not an end date. You could choose to leave that value NULL. Another approach is to say, "the value is valid from now until the end of time", so you could add a value that represents the end of time. That might be 9999-12-31. While it is a type of what I would call a "magic" value, I am happy with either mechanism being used.

The end of time value certainly makes it easier to write SQL queries as BETWEEN clauses will then work, unlike NULL values.

If you do decide to have an end of time value rather than NULL, make sure that you do not use automatic calendars in Power BI. You might end up with a very, very large list of dates in your analytic model.

Missing Rows

Imagine that are loading a series of invoices, into your data warehouse table, and each invoice needs to refer to a customer. Now, further imagine that when you look up the customer to find their key, no such customer exists.

How can that happen?

There are many possible reasons but here are some:

- You are loading the data in batches, and for some reason, you are loading the invoices before you load the customers. For this reason, I always have a loading order for tables, to maximize the chance that this sort of issue will not arise. It might, however, be that you tried to load the customers first, but something went wrong during that process.

- You are trickle-feeding incremental changes into the system, and the source system is processing changes out of order.

- The source system is simply faulty. It has no referential integrity that checks for these errors, and they are being passed onto the data warehouse.

The question is then: what do you do about this?

One option is to put the rows that do not match in another location until the problem is sorted out. This is a poor idea. This will tend to build a growing mess and it often never gets resolved. Worse, if invoices are being categorized by not only customers, but products, dates, and more, then all the analytics are now wrong, not just the categorization by customers.

A second option is to set the ones that do not match to a specific "Unknown Customer" or "Unknown Product" key, etc. While this gives valid analytics because all the rows are present, there is no obvious way that the issue will be resolved when the real data finally appears.

A third option is to "infer" that a customer must have existed. You could create a row in the Customers table based upon whatever information you have in the incoming data for the invoices. At least it will have a business key (or ID or Code). In these designs, I used to add an IsInferred column to indicate that the row was inferred in this way. Then when the "real" customer data arrived, the row would just be updated rather than versioned.

In older designs with multidimensional models, I used this inference of rows quite regularly. It worked well unless there was a problem with the source system. It was important to keep monitoring the number of inferred rows to make sure it was not growing constantly.

Today, I do not need to do this. Multidimensional analytic models needed this for consistency, but today I use tabular analytic models in almost every project, and they deal quite well with missing rows. In the tabular models, a blank customer or blank product would automatically be added when a customer row or a product row is missing. I like the way that this works, and no extra effort is required in the design and/or monitoring.

Lineage

For your analytics to be meaningful, the users must believe that the values you are presenting to them are correct. I often see analytic systems that look great, but when the users look at the data, they say:

"I do not believe that number"

And then what do you do? In many cases, several systems provide the source data, and the data has then been loaded, and transformed. It might not be immediately obvious where the data came from. One option that can help to alleviate this problem is to ensure that you record lineage information in your DataModel tables.

If I am loading data in batches periodically, I often then create a table called DataModel.Lineages, with a schema like this:

```
CREATE TABLE DataModel.Lineages
(
    LineageKey int NOT NULL
        CONSTRAINT PK_DataModel_Lineages PRIMARY KEY
        CONSTRAINT DF_DataModel_Lineages_LineageKey
            DEFAULT (NEXT VALUE FOR DataModel.LineageKey),
    LoadDateTime datetime2(3) NOT NULL,
    LoadingProcess nvarchar(200) NOT NULL,
    LoadingIdentity sysname NOT NULL,
    SourceSystem nvarchar(200) NULL
);
```

Every time I load a batch of data, I add a row to this table. I then add the LineageKey to the rows that were inserted or updated in the other DataModel tables.

If the table will not be visible within the analytics, I would create it in the DataLoad schema instead.

The columns that I use will vary from project to project, but in the example above I have used:

- LoadDateTime – I need to know when the loading occurred. If the extraction from the source system happened at a very different time to when the loading into the DataModel tables happened, those extracts will be tracked as well.

- LoadingProcess – I need to know which process loaded the data. In some cases, there are multiple data paths that can insert or update the DataModel tables. Often this will be the name of a stored procedure, but it could be an SSIS package or other processes.

- LoadingIdentity – I need to know the identity that was being used by the loading process. This will usually be an Azure AD or Windows identity. it is important to know this as different identities might receive different output for the same query against a source system.

- SourceSystem – If there are multiple source systems used by the process, it might be helpful to know which one was involved in this data.

Table Compression

When you ask most IT people about storage compression, they assume it has two characteristics:

- It reduces the size

- It makes it operations much slower

That is because they have had previous experience with the disk compression schemes that were used in Windows. And sadly, it is the primary reason why so many have never tried table compression in SQL Server. The secondary reason was that until SQL Server 2016, table compression was only offered in the Enterprise Edition of SQL Server.

Let me make it clear: **table compression makes your tables smaller and faster, not slower**.

Row Compression

There are two types of table compression: row compression and page compression. With row compression, all that changes is the way that each row's data is stored on the storage pages. For example, values that are fixed length can become variable length to save space. Other values can be stored in the number of bits required, not the full allocated size. The effect is that more rows fit in each page.

I find that in most transactional systems that I work with, row compression reduces the size of tables around 30%. While you might think that space is not an issue for you, it is important to realize that for most SQL Server systems today, IO is the bottleneck, not CPU. Anything you do to reduce the amount of IO that is occurring is a good thing. Reducing IO by 30% can have a profound impact.

But the benefits do not stop there. Pages are stored in memory buffers the same way. That means that you now fit more than 1/3 more data in the same amount of system memory. This can also have a powerful impact in further reducing IO.

What is the catch?

Some documentation points out that you have a slight increase in CPU when you are using compression. My experience shows that the overall CPU load can decrease as well. The reason for that, is that while the CPU effort per-page is increased, the overall number of pages has decreased significantly.

I can only strongly encourage you to use row compression as a default on both your transactional systems, and your data warehouses. When I first set this up at most customer sites, they are simply amazed that they had not tried it before.

Page Compression

The other form of compression is page compression. It takes the compression on a page further. Instead of compressing a single row, it uses the data from multiple rows to achieve higher levels of compression. When using page compression, I often see a 75% reduction in the size of tables, or even more. Tables are often just over 20% of their original size.

Why do not I use this everywhere?

The problem with page compression is that it significantly increases the work required to modify data on the page. If you use page compression on tables that are heavily modified, you can impact your overall performance significantly.

I tend to use a blend of row and page compression. I use row compression as a default, and I use page compression on tables (and indexes) where the rows are scanned more than 80% of the time and updated less than 20% of the time. Clearly that takes some investigative work, but the benefits can be profound if you get this right.

Columnstore Indexes

There is a third type of compression that can be applied to tables. A table can have a columnstore index. This is like the way that tabular data models work in Analysis Services and Power BI.

While columnstores can have an even greater impact on compression (I often see tables 10% of their original size), and read performance when you are scanning the table, they can have an even greater impact when you are modifying data, particularly if you are doing that row by row.

Columnstores can be part of your data warehouse, but they require careful design.

Chapter 6: Implementing the Analytics Schema

Overview

In my designs, the Analytics schema is the one that is presented to analytic tools like Analysis Services, Tableau, Power BI Premium and more.

I also use it as a security barrier for the database.

Awesome image by Raymond Pang

Analytics Schema in the Data Warehouse Structure

I mentioned previously that I separate all our logic into a series of schemas. The overall flow of the data is as follows:

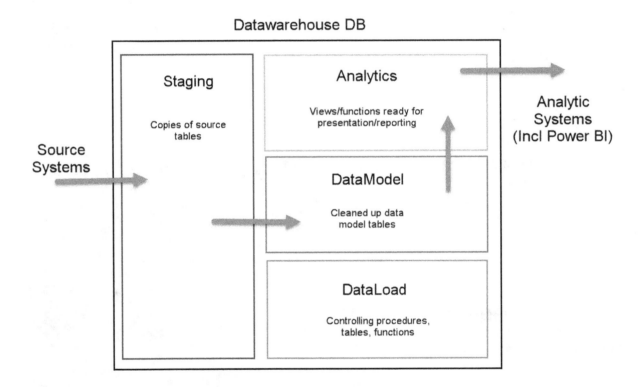

Source system data is usually from another database, or it might be from a series of files. No matter where it comes from, I start by bringing the data into a **Staging** schema.

In the last chapter, I discussed the **DataModel** schema. It contains cleansed and transformed data. The data in the DataModel schema is ready to be consumed, and ready to be stored longer term if that is required.

The **Analytics** schema is a series of views (and occasionally functions) that are ready to be consumed by analytic tools like Analysis Services or Power BI. Apart from keys, the names are human readable and presentable, without the need for further renaming. I also use this schema as a security boundary.

The process of orchestrating the moving and cleansing of data is performed by the objects in the **DataLoad** schema. They are usually stored procedures and functions but might also involve tables for meta-data driven automation, or for reference and mapping tables.

I will look at the other schemas later, but in this chapter, you will see how I structure the Analytics schema.

Analytics Schema Design Goals

I used the Analytics schema as the point of connection for:

- Tabular data model loading

- Reporting Services connections (if being used for strategic reporting)

- Power BI direct query connections (if used – but I tend to use SSAS with live connection instead)

Minimizing the Attack Surface

It is important to limit access to your databases from higher level applications and services. Unfortunately, organizations that have had breaches do not tend to talk about them publicly. They are usually embarrassed about them and concerned about the organization's reputation.

In my consulting work, I get to see the aftermath of breaches at a variety of organizations.

When you are working with security, hoping for the best is not an appropriate plan.

Every time I go to a Power BI or reporting presentation, and I see the presenter writing T-SQL queries directly into the reporting tool, or even just loading tables directly into the reporting tool, I cringe. Invariably, they are using a connection that can read whatever it wants from within the database.

That is not a reasonable security posture.

Instead, I do the following:

- Create a schema called Analytics.

- Add to the schema the views that the analytic and/or reporting tools need to access. There might also be functions and stored procedures but mostly for these, I am only using views.

- Ensure that no other objects (like tables) are placed into the Analytics schema.

- Create a role that is used for analytics.

- Grant the role SELECT and EXECUTE permissions on the Analytics schema, and no other permissions.

- Add the user that the analytics or reporting tool is connecting as to the role that I created.

By doing this, I know that if any intrusion or breach occurs in the analytic or reporting tool, that at the very most, the breach will allow access to these views, and nothing else.

The same applies to organizational websites. I would rather create a WebSite schema and put into it, just the objects that the website is permitted to use. Far too many developers assume that the web application should have complete access to underlying databases.

Embedding T-SQL

I mentioned a moment ago that I see presentations where the person demoing the code, is entering T-SQL directly into Power BI or into reporting tools.

No matter how simple that appears to be, do not do this.

I go into organizations all the time, where the people looking after the databases feel like they can never make any changes at all.

Why?

Because they have zero visibility into all the code that touches the database. When there is T-SQL code embedded in reports, PBIX files, Excel spreadsheets, Access DBs, or code built on the fly in applications, it is impossible to understand the dependencies involved.

All the database people know is that if they change something in the database, someone is likely to yell at them, but they do not know who that will be before they make the change. So, they get to the point where they are not prepared to change anything.

Ironically, the developers at these same organizations will tell me that they had to do it this way, to be sufficiently agile. Yet, what they end up building is the exact opposite of agility.

Far better to have at least one layer of abstraction in the database and use it as a contract for interaction with the relevant applications.

Outcome of the Analytics Schema

I have discussed that the Analytics schema is where analytic tools like Analysis Services, and Power BI connect. I have a few aims for this schema:

1. The security boundary that I have just discussed.

2. The naming in the views is ready for consumption, without needing to be renamed in the analytic tools i.e., the names are already human-readable and human-presentable.

Excluding DataModel Data

When I create a view for the Analytics schema, I often do not include all the data that is in the underlying DataModel table. That usually occurs for one of three reasons:

- The DataModel table might contain a large amount of history and the analytics work only requires recent data.

- The DataModel table might contain a large amount of history that is not required in the analytics. I might also have recent data in detail, but older data aggregated (summarized).

- I might have columns in the DataModel tables that are needed for other types of reporting but are not required in the analytic models. I have been working with timber quite a bit lately and for each stick, there is a set of readings. They are needed for some reporting but have zero value in a tabular analytic model.

Design Rules

The following diagram shows an example of views in the Analytics schema:

```
□ ▦ Views
    ⊞ ▦ System Views
    ⊞ 🗗 Analytics.Business Category
    ⊞ 🗗 Analytics.Business Category Special Price
    ⊞ 🗗 Analytics.Buying Group
    □ 🗗 Analytics.Buying Group Special Price
        □ ▦ Columns
            🗎 BuyingGroupSpecialPriceKey (int, not null)
            🗎 BuyingGroupKey (int, not null)
            🗎 StockItemKey (int, not null)
            🗎 Discount Percentage (decimal(18,3), not null)
            🗎 Discount Amount (decimal(18,2), not null)
            🗎 Established Date (date, not null)
            🗎 Cost at Time (decimal(18,2), not null)
            🗎 Is Price Override (bit, not null)
            🗎 Promotion Start Date (date, not null)
            🗎 Promotion End Date (date, not null)
        ⊞ ▦ Triggers
        ⊞ ▦ Indexes
        ⊞ ▦ Statistics
    ⊞ 🗗 Analytics.Customer
    ⊞ 🗗 Analytics.Customer Backorder
```

I have simple design rules for these views:

- The views generally just reformat the naming from DataModel tables

- I use singular table names in this schema

- Column names are ready for use in reports and analytics

- For all displayable columns, names contain spaces to separate words

- Simple linking words like "at", "in", "of", etc. are not capitalized. In the example above, you can see there is a "Cost at Time" column that was derived from the underlying CostAtTime column in the DataModel table.

- Key columns remain PascalCased without spaces.

- Words like "Percentage" can be replaced with symbols like "%" if preferred. In the example above, "Discount Percentage" could have been "Discount %".

Automating View Creation

Wherever possible, I try to automate the creation of code. I like the old saying that it is better to write code that writes code, than to just write code.

To create the views in the Analytics schema, there is a tool in our free SDU Tools (https://sdutools.sqldownunder.com) called **ScriptAnalyticsViewInCurrentDatabase**.

Let us look at an example of using this tool. I will start with an example table from the DataModel schema:

```
DROP TABLE IF EXISTS DataModel.CustomerSpecialPrices;
GO

CREATE TABLE DataModel.CustomerSpecialPrices
(
    CustomerSpecialPriceKey int NOT NULL
        CONSTRAINT PK_DataModel_CustomerSpecialPrices PRIMARY KEY
        CONSTRAINT DF_DataModel_CustomerSpecialPrices_CustomerSpecialPriceKey
            DEFAULT (NEXT VALUE FOR DataModel.CustomerSpecialPriceKey),
    CustomerKey int NOT NULL,
    StockItemKey int NOT NULL,
    DiscountPercentage decimal(18, 3) NOT NULL,
    DiscountAmount decimal(18, 2) NOT NULL,
    EstablishedDate date NOT NULL,
    CostAtTime decimal(18, 2) NOT NULL,
    IsPriceOverride bit NOT NULL,
    PromotionStartDate date NOT NULL,
    PromotionEndDate date NOT NULL
);
GO
```

I could just start writing a view definition for this table, but in this case, I will use the ScriptAnalyticsViewInCurrentDatabase tool instead. To do that, I execute the following code:

```
DECLARE @SQL nvarchar(max);

EXEC SDU_Tools.ScriptAnalyticsViewInCurrentDatabase
    @TableSchemaName = N'DataModel',
    @TableName = N'CustomerSpecialPrices',
    @ViewSchemaName = N'Analytics',
    @ViewName = N'CustomerSpecialPrice',
    @ScriptOutput = @SQL OUTPUT;

EXEC SDU_Tools.ExecuteOrPrint @SQL;
```

Note how the table and view names are specified. Basically, you need to supply:

- The source schema. In my case, that will almost always be DataModel

- The source table name. In this example I have used the CustomerSpecialPrices table

- The schema for the output view. In my case, that will almost always be Analytics

- The view name. For this parameter, pass the singular name of the source table. In this example, that is CustomerSpecialPrice. Note that I did not include spaces in this parameter value.

- @ScriptOutput is the variable that will hold the script that is created.

After executing this code in my sample BeanPerfection database, the output is:

```
CREATE OR ALTER VIEW Analytics.[Customer Special Price]
AS
SELECT CustomerSpecialPriceKey,
       CustomerKey,
       StockItemKey,
       DiscountPercentage AS [Discount Percentage],
       DiscountAmount AS [Discount Amount],
       EstablishedDate AS [Established Date],
       CostAtTime AS [Cost At Time],
       IsPriceOverride AS [Is Price Override],
       PromotionStartDate AS [Promotion Start Date],
       PromotionEndDate AS [Promotion End Date]
FROM DataModel.CustomerSpecialPrices;
GO
```

This output is almost what I want. Keys are left unchanged. Other columns are spaced out. The only thing that I am likely to change is "Cost At Time". I will change that to "Cost at Time" before I create it. (There is a chance that I will change the tool in the future to do this automatically).

Either way, the tool has done the hard work in writing the code for the view. I hope you find it useful.

Installing SDU Tools

If you want to use these SDU Tools, you can find them at https://sdutools.sqldownunder.com. They are free to use for anyone who is a member of our SDU Insiders email list. (It is a very low volume list).

SDU Tools install themselves in a single schema called SDU_Tools.

I create updates to the tools many times each year.

When you download the tools, you will receive a zip file that contains several SQL scripts:

- A script to install SDU Tools in a SQL Server database

- A script to install SDU Tools in an Azure SQL Database

- A script to remove SDU Tools in a SQL Server database

- A script to remove SDU Tools in an Azure SQL Database

- A script that demonstrates recently-added functionality

Date Tables or Views

Data models almost always need a table of dates. It is a rare analytic model that is not interested in when something happened. There are two ways that I implement a table of dates:

- Create a DataModel.Dates table and an Analytics.Date view

- Just create an Analytics.Date view

I prefer creating the underlying DataModel.Dates table. Either way, I limit the range of dates based upon the data that is in the other DataModel tables. When I do this, it is important to index the DataModel tables to make it quick to detect the required range of dates.

Note that analytic tools like Power BI can create automatically created date tables or calendars. There are many aspects of them that I do not like, and I do not use them.

Automating Date Table Creation

There are three functions in the SDU Tools toolset that can make it easy to generate date tables.

- DatesBetween

- DateDimensionColumns

- DateDimensionPeriodColumns

The DatesBetween function takes a from date and a to date and returns all the dates between those dates.

The DateDimensionColumns function returns many columns that are useful in date tables (or date dimensions).

The DateDimensionPeriodColumns function adds many more columns that can be useful but based upon periods. For example, there are columns that tell you if the row is today, or yesterday, or the next working day, or is the start or end of a financial period.

At the very least, these functions should give you examples of how to write the SQL code that is needed.

The general structure of the SQL code for using these functions is as follows:

```
CREATE OR ALTER VIEW Analytics.[Date]
AS
SELECT db.DateValue AS [Date],
       db.RequiredColumns,
       ddc.RequiredColumns,
       ddps.RequiredColumns
FROM SDU_Tools.DatesBetween
(
    (SELECT MIN(SomeDate) FROM DataModel.RelevantRows),
    (SELECT MAX(SomeDate) FROM DataModel.RelevantRows)
) AS db
CROSS APPLY SDU_Tools.DateDimensionColumns (db.DateValue, 7) AS ddc
CROSS APPLY SDU_Tools.DateDimensionPeriodColumns (db.DateValue, 7, SYSDATETIME()) AS ddpc;
GO
```

Local DateTime in Azure SQL Database

I work a lot with Azure SQL Database, and if you have done that, you will have realised that, just like other Azure services, the time zone is set to UTC. Select from GETDATE() or SYSDATETIME(), and you will find it is the current UTC date and time i.e., the same as you would get from the SYSUTCDATETIME() function.

I can see why that makes sense much of the time. If your users are all over the world, that seems an entirely appropriate setting. Same logic if you are linking different systems together: it is good to have a common timeframe.

However, if all your users are in, say Sydney, suddenly that seems to be a problem. All the users are going to want to use Sydney time. I wish there was a way to set the time zone for an Azure SQL Database but currently, there is not.

111

sys.time_zone_info

In SQL Server 2016, Microsoft added a new system view called **sys.time_zone_info**. If you query it, you can see what it does:

```
SELECT * FROM sys.time_zone_info;
```

110 %

Results | Messages

	name	current_utc_offset	is_currently_dst
1	Dateline Standard Time	-12:00	0
2	UTC-11	-11:00	0
3	Aleutian Standard Time	-09:00	1
4	Hawaiian Standard Time	-10:00	0
5	Marquesas Standard Time	-09:30	0
6	Alaskan Standard Time	-08:00	1
7	UTC-09	-09:00	0
8	Pacific Standard Time (Mexico)	-07:00	1
9	UTC-08	-08:00	0
10	Pacific Standard Time	-07:00	1
11	US Mountain Standard Time	-07:00	0

It has time zones and their current UTC offset, and lets you know if the time zone currently daylight has saving time.

Note that this is not giving you historical info. That is a much harder problem. It is just the value at the current time.

Current Local Time

Now in theory, I could use this to get the current local time for a given timezone:

```sql
USE tempdb;
GO

CREATE OR ALTER FUNCTION dbo.CurrentLocalTime
(
    @TimeZoneName sysname
)
RETURNS datetime2
AS
BEGIN
--
-- Test examples:
/*
SELECT dbo.CurrentLocalTime('AUS Eastern Standard Time');
*/
  RETURN DATEADD(hour,
  TRY_CAST((SELECT REPLACE(current_utc_offset, N':', N'.')
      FROM sys.time_zone_info
      WHERE [name] = @TimeZoneName) AS decimal(18,2)),
      SYSDATETIME());
END;
GO
```

The challenge with this, is it is way, way too slow. I have also found it leads to poor estimates in query plans. Now while the SQL Server team has done great work with T-SQL scalar functions lately, this function would still have performance issues, and restrict parallelism. Based on that, I would not recommend calling it for every row in a large rowset.

AT TIME ZONE

So, let us look at a faster option. If you are comfortable with including a larger (and less obvious) expression directly into your code in place of GETDATE() or SYSDATETIME(), you can create a better performing expression by using the AT TIME ZONE modifier that was added in SQL Server 2016.

You can use SYSDATETIMEOFFSET() to retrieve the current date, time, and offset at the server, and then use AT TIME ZONE to change the value to the target time zone. Then, because you no doubt want a date, a datetime or datetime2 value (rather than a datetimeoffset), you will need to CAST it to what you need.

For example, if you want the current date and time as a datetime value like GETDATE() does, do this:

CAST(SYSDATETIMEOFFSET() AT TIME ZONE 'AUS Eastern Standard Time' AS datetime)

If you want the current date and time as a datetime2 value like SYSDATETIME() does, do this:

CAST(SYSDATETIMEOFFSET() AT TIME ZONE 'AUS Eastern Standard Time' AS datetime2)

And if you just want the current date, you can do this:

CAST(SYSDATETIMEOFFSET() AT TIME ZONE 'AUS Eastern Standard Time' AS date)

I know it is wordier and far less obvious to someone reading the code than the function, but it will perform better. So, if performance matters, this will be a better option.

Automatic Data Subsetting

If you have worked with larger tables in either Power BI, Analysis Services, or any analytic tool, you will know that developing against them is painful. Any time the data needs to be refreshed (which happens often), you spend a lot of time sitting around waiting for it to happen.

A friend of mine who works for Microsoft, Chris Webb proposed a way of getting sampled data during development. It was interesting, and I saw that fellow MVP Marc Lelijveld also uses a similar method.

In both cases though, they are using a TOP N inserted in their queries to limit the number of rows. But that has never been what I want.

What I Want to Achieve

First, I do not really want a TOP N, as I generally want a specific range of dates. For example, while I might want all data when the model is in production, or I might have a starting date for that, I usually want just a specific subset of the data for development. I often want, say, just the last two months.

Second, when I am working with source control systems, I do not want to be changing the BIM or PBIX files in any way at all, as they move between development and deployment. I do not even want to use different parameters.

Ideally, I wish the development tools like PBI Desktop, Analysis Services Tabular Designer in Visual Studio, etc. automagically included an extra limiting predicate while I am developing.

My Workaround

In the meantime, I have come up with what I think is a pretty good workaround. I am making the views that I connect to, determine what to return, based on either the HOST_NAME() or APP_NAME() functions based on the SQL Server connection. Let me show you.

First, I will create a table to hold a list of the hosts that I am using for development:

```
DROP TABLE IF EXISTS DataModel.DevelopmentHosts;
GO

CREATE TABLE DataModel.DevelopmentHosts
(
    DevelopmentHostID int IDENTITY(1,1)
        CONSTRAINT PK_DataModel_DevelopmentHosts
            PRIMARY KEY,
    HostName sysname NOT NULL
);
GO

CREATE INDEX IX_DataModel_DevelopmentHosts_HostName
ON DataModel.DevelopmentHosts (HostName);
GO
```

Note: I often get questions about the data type **sysname**. It is the data type for system objects, and is currently mapped to nvarchar(128).

Next, I will create and populate a table that I am pretending is part of my data model:

```sql
DROP TABLE IF EXISTS DataModel.Transactions;
GO

CREATE TABLE DataModel.Transactions
(
    TransactionID bigint IDENTITY(1,1)
        CONSTRAINT PK_DataModel_Transactions
            PRIMARY KEY,
    TransactionDate date NOT NULL,
    TransactionAmount decimal(18,2) NOT NULL,
    IsFinalised bit NOT NULL
);
GO

SET NOCOUNT ON;

DECLARE @DateCounter date = DATEADD(year, -1, SYSDATETIME());

WHILE @DateCounter < SYSDATETIME()
BEGIN
    INSERT DataModel.Transactions
    (
        TransactionDate, TransactionAmount, IsFinalised
    )
    VALUES (@DateCounter, RAND(12) * 100.0, 0);

    SET @DateCounter = DATEADD(day, 1, @DateCounter);
END;
GO
```

In the example, I have added a transaction for every day in the last year.

Next, I will create the type of analytic view that we often use:

```sql
CREATE OR ALTER VIEW Analytics.[Transaction]
AS
SELECT t.TransactionDate AS [Transaction Date],
        t.TransactionAmount AS [Transaction Amount],
        t.IsFinalised AS [Is Finalised]
FROM DataModel.Transactions AS t
      -- normal start date for this table
WHERE t.TransactionDate >= '19900101';
GO
```

This view has a hard cutoff date for loading data (perhaps the start of sensible data) and if I query this view, I see all 365 rows.

Subsetting the Data

What I am then doing is changing the view so that it makes decisions based on working out if I am in development or not:

```
CREATE OR ALTER VIEW Analytics.[Transaction]
AS
SELECT t.TransactionDate AS [Transaction Date],
       t.TransactionAmount AS [Transaction Amount],
       t.IsFinalised AS [Is Finalised]
FROM DataModel.Transactions AS t
WHERE t.TransactionDate >=
    CASE WHEN EXISTS (SELECT 1 FROM DataModel.DevelopmentHosts
                                 WHERE HostName = HOST_NAME())
            -- development subset for this table
         THEN DATEADD(month, -2, SYSDATETIME())
            -- normal date range for this table
         ELSE '19900101' -- normal date for this table
    END;
GO
```

If the query is not coming from a development host, it will return all data since the same hard-coded start date (i.e., start of 1990). But if I am on a development host, it will just return the last two months of data.

To see this, I will add my client to the list of development hosts:

```
INSERT DataModel.DevelopmentHosts
(
    HostName
)
VALUES (HOST_NAME());
GO
```

When I query the same view again, now I see only 62 rows, without changing the code at all.

Back in Power BI or Analysis Services Tabular Designer, if I am on my client, I see the subset, but on the server, I see all the data without changing the BIM or PBIX file at all.

There might be situations where making the choice based upon the host name just won't work for you. In that case, I would suggest checking the APP_NAME() function instead of the HOST_NAME() function, and having a list of apps that get development subsets instead of full data sets.

Chapter 7: Using DevOps for Project Management and Deployment

Overview

It is important to have good control over your projects. There are many tools that you could be using, but one of my favorites at present is Azure DevOps.

It provides both project management capabilities, but also Git-based source control, and provides a good solution for continuous integration (CI) and continuous deployment (CD).

In this chapter, I will introduce how you might use it as part of your implementation of Power BI and analytics in an enterprise.

Awesome image by Ben Kolde

Project Management and Deployment Goals

For any project management and deployment tooling that I use, I have some core goals:

- I need a great source control system, and nowadays, that means a Git-based system

- I need to be able to create repeatable processes. These are critical to being able to produce repeatable high-quality outcomes.

- I need to be able to support multiple environments. Tools that only support a single state of the system are not useful. With environment support, I can have Development, Test, UAT (User Acceptance Testing), Production, etc. The list of environments at each site might differ but the need for environments is important.

- I need a way to manage the tasks that are being performed as the systems are being developed. At a minimum, this usually involves some form of Kanban Board.

Once the core goals are met, I then have a few other desirable goals:

- I want to be able to build databases and other code using continuous integration (CI).

- I want reliable deployment of the outcomes to different environments using continuous deployment (CD).

- For a bonus, I would like to have a tool to manage testing.

Azure DevOps

Microsoft today has two core offerings in this area: Azure DevOps, and GitHub. There are pros and cons of each, and I will discuss those later in this chapter. I believe that (at the time of writing), the easiest way to get started, especially for new teams, is to use Azure DevOps.

The motto for the Azure DevOps teams was to "turn ideas into software". They stated their goals as:

- Plan smarter

- Collaborate better

- Create quality

- Ship faster

Azure DevOps is a web-based suite of tools and services to help you build applications of many types, including those types that I need for implementing Power BI analytics in enterprises. It is low-cost yet powerful tooling and can integrate with your on-premises work where necessary and can also integrate with a large variety of third-party (non-Microsoft) tools.

At the time of writing, for up to five users, Azure DevOps was basically free.

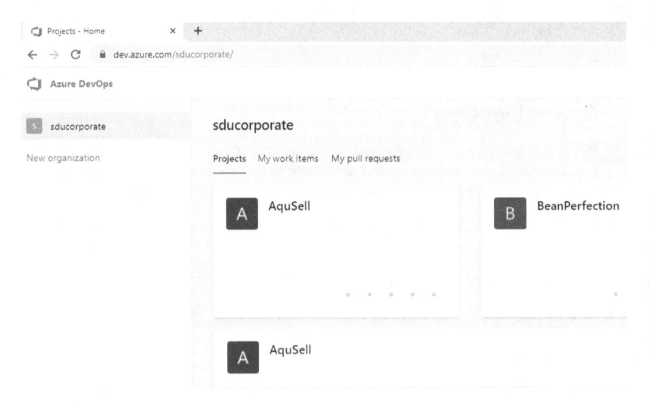

The top-level object in Azure DevOps is an Organization. This usually equates well to a real-world organization. The next level down is the Project. In the screenshot above, you can see the home page with an AquSell project and a BeanPerfection project.

I like the way that projects work in Azure DevOps. You can assign team members to a project and give them permissions within the project. But importantly, you can also have multiple repositories (of code and other objects) within a project. GitHub currently lacks this level and goes straight from an Enterprise level to a Repository level. Most of my projects need multiple repositories.

Project Wiki

At the project level, you can also have a Project Wiki. This can be useful for documentation related to that project. It is hosted within a repository and written in Markdown. The flavor of Markdown used is closely related to the GitHub variant, and supports some of the common Mermaid diagrams.

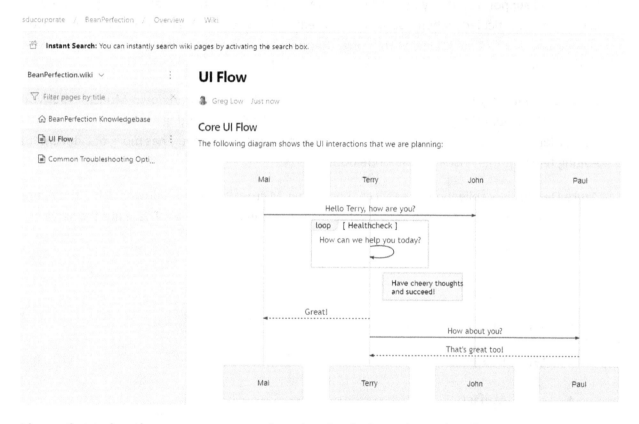

I know that today, there are so many tools and technologies to learn, but if you are not familiar with Markdown, I would suggest you become familiar with it. It has fast become the de facto way that documentation is written and maintained.

Markdown allows you to have rich text formats displayed but supported by plain text. This makes it especially powerful when you need to compare versions of documentation over time and see what has changed. Comparing plain text is orders of magnitude easier than comparing, say, Microsoft Word documents.

If Mermaid supports all that you need for diagrams and charts, again these are easy to compare across time, particularly when you compare them to images in bitmap formats like png. If you change one word on an image, with a png, it appears that the entire image has changed. With Mermaid, you can see exactly which word has changed.

For a long time, my favorite tool for editing Markdown has been Markdown Monster, but you should not discount Visual Studio Code. It is free and works well for editing Markdown, particularly when Mermaid diagrams are being used. Markdown Monster, however, has more of a document editing feel to it than Visual Studio Code does.

Azure DevOps is a collection of services. I note that Microsoft has been downplaying the Azure DevOps name in favor of all the individual service names in recent times. These are the services:

- Azure Boards

- Azure Repos

- Azure Pipelines

- Azure Test Plans

- Azure Artifacts

Azure Monitor and Azure Log Analytics are not part of these tools but are also closely associated with them. In the following section, I will provide you an introduction to each of these services.

Azure Boards

Azure Boards is a service that provides Kanban style boards for tracking the progress of a project. It can be configured in different ways, but it directly supports the most common Agile/Scrum requirements.

Azure Boards lets you track workitems and tasks and be able to see the backlogs that exist. Importantly, when you make changes to code in the source repositories, you can link those code changes directly to workitems.

The workitems can be assigned to specific sprints.

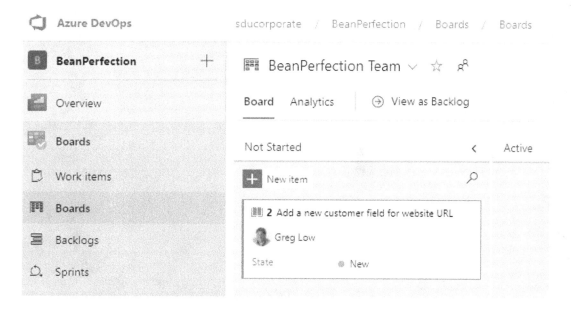

Azure Boards provides configurable team dashboards, and you can create custom reports. For users, many standard queries are provided but it is also easy to create custom queries and then save those queries for re-use.

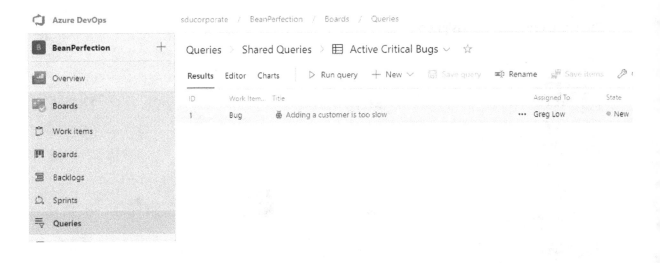

Azure Repos

Azure Repos is a private Git-based hosted repository. There are currently no limits on the number of repositories or of the size of each repository that you can use.

As it is Git-based, it works well with existing Git clients.

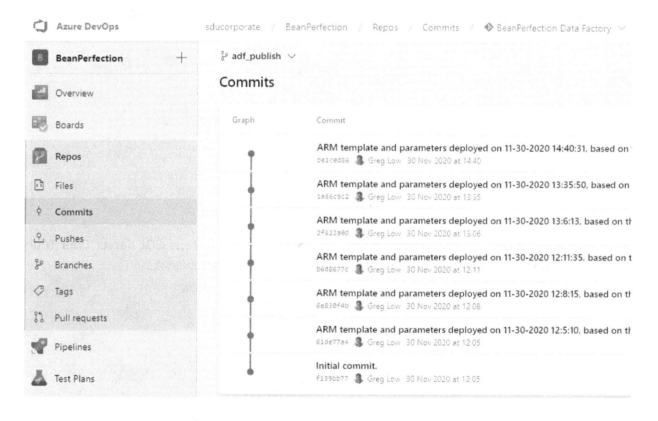

As mentioned earlier, I like the way that I can have multiple repositories closely associated with each other within a single project:

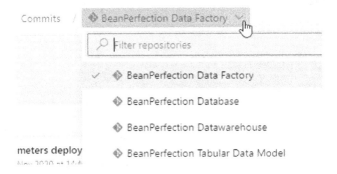

Azure Repos integrates smoothly with both Visual Studio (where I use SQL Server Data Tools projects) and Azure Data Factory (which I regularly use for integration work).

Azure Pipelines

Azure Pipelines is used to orchestrate both building and deploying code.

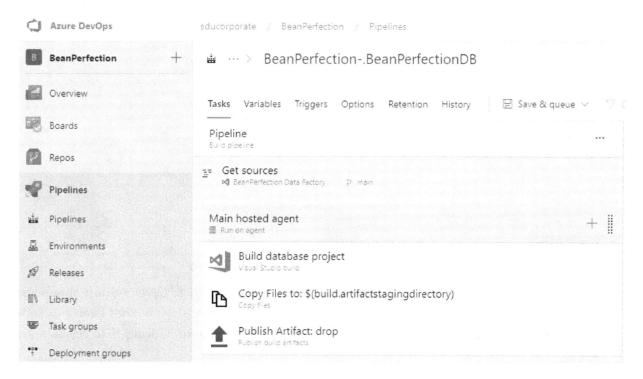

While it can perform very complex builds when required, and control on-premises build agents, for most of my analytics projects, the needs are straightforward. Generally, I use a build pipeline to perform a build on my database projects. The build agent is a hosted agent provided by Microsoft, and so if I have a database project in an Azure repo, I can have it built without me needing to provide other systems and resources. The output of that build is a DACPAC file. That is referred to as a published artifact from the build process.

Deployment is performed by what is called a Release Pipeline. In the diagram, you can see the incoming artifacts on the left. For a database, that is the DACPAC file that was build. Then there are Stages. For my projects, these equate to environments that I am deploying to.

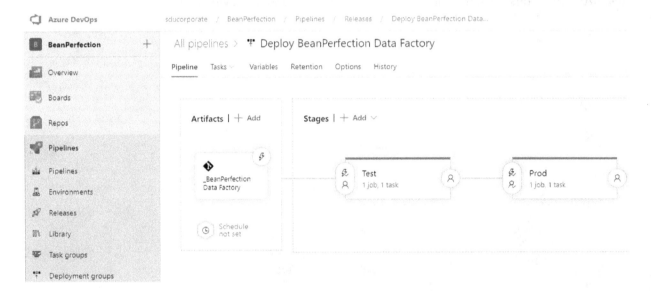

The release pipelines also offer very rich functionality, like the ability to have pre/post approvals. This means that I can automatically deploy to Test, and once the deployment has been checked, someone with authority can authorize the deployment that will automatically then continue to Prod.

Azure Pipelines is language agnostic. It can build a Java application and deploy to Linux, just as easily as you can build and deploy database code or .NET code.

It is also highly extensible. There is an Azure DevOps marketplace where there are both free and paid extensions that have been provided by third parties.

It is important to learn to work with these types of tools. You need reliable and repeatable outcomes.

Infrastructure as Code

Many years ago, I used to teach a lot of Microsoft Official Curriculum courses. Each course had a detailed and complex setup required for each student PC. Depending upon the technician at each training center's abilities, it was rare for all the machines in the room to be configured the same way, although, in theory, the same setup instructions were followed.

As soon as humans get involved in the deployments and configuration, there is a much higher chance of configuration errors creeping in. Yet I still go to so many customer sites where, when they need say a new virtual machine, a technician in the company starts installing and configuring the operating system.

You should no longer be doing this.

Infrastructure as Code (IaC) is an important concept. Instead of representing the configuration of a system as a set of instructions to follow, you should consider the configuration of the system as code that ends up in source control, and is versioned, etc. as with any other code. Machines should then be deployed from this code. If you do this, it is then easy to deploy new environments as required, as part of your release pipelines.

Azure Test Plans

I have a strong preference for automated testing wherever possible. Most automated testing should be performed as part of either:

- Code check-in

- Continuous integration builds

It is important to give feedback to developers as early in the development cycle as possible. If there are checks that can be made every time, they check-in code, that can provide rapid feedback.

There are other issues that will only be found when the overall project is built. Perhaps an object is missing. This feedback can be provided when a build is performed.

Apart from the developer testing though, there might be a need to manage manual testing that is performed later, usually after deployment. Azure Test Plans can provide this.

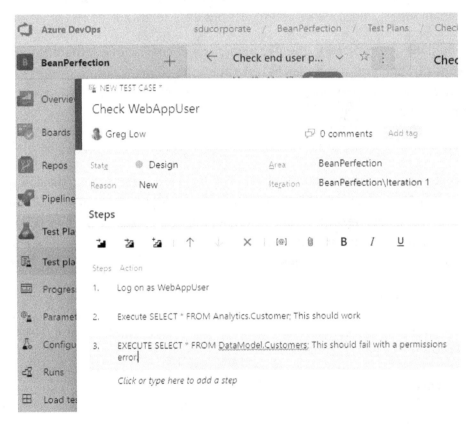

I can create a test plan that I want performed, then specify the steps that should be followed in the plan. At each point, I can specify what should and should not work. This helps to provide end-to-end traceability for the code you build. For example, you might have steps to walk through using a Power BI report that you have built, to make sure it works as the users expected.

Azure Artifacts

This tooling is less likely to be used in building Power BI and analytics code, but it still might be relevant.

Many projects have a dependency on external code. In fact, estimates suggest that more than 90% of code in corporate applications is from open-source libraries. Even in Power BI, you are likely to be using custom visuals.

If you have many developers, how do you know that they are all using the same version of the visuals? What will you do if the third-party site that you were using code from, suddenly disappears?

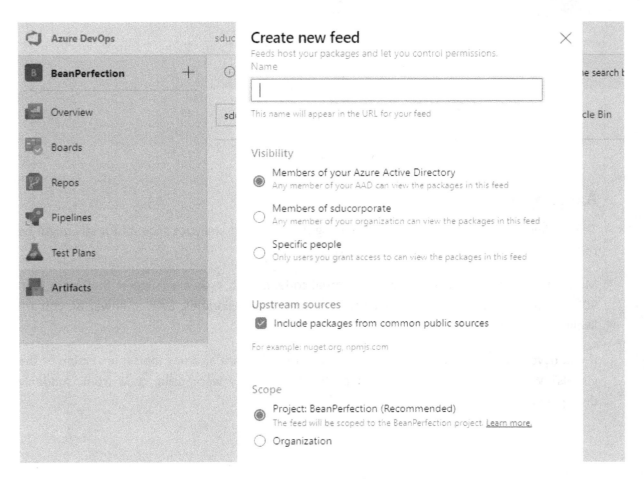

Azure Artifacts allows you to control the source of dependencies. You can repackage the dependencies that you have approved for use and provide a feed that developers can use to obtain the external code.

Azure Monitor / Azure Log Analytics

When your applications and systems are in use, it is important to collect telemetry and logs about how they are performing. For example, how busy is your SQL database? Are queries ever timing out.

Azure has a concept of "Insights". These are built-in bundles of telemetry that you can add to applications and services. For example, "SQL Insights" can collect information from Azure SQL Database as it is being used.

This data will be stored in Azure Log Analytics. This location can also be used to store logs from a wide variety of sources. If you have virtual machines, you can have system logs from those machines also stored in Azure Log Analytics.

To make it easy to query this data, Azure Monitor provides the ability to monitor metrics and to create alerts. For example, if one of my Azure Data Factory pipelines fails, I can configure an alert to let me know that this has happened. But I might also want an alert if a server is more than 90% busy for longer than 10 minutes, and so on.

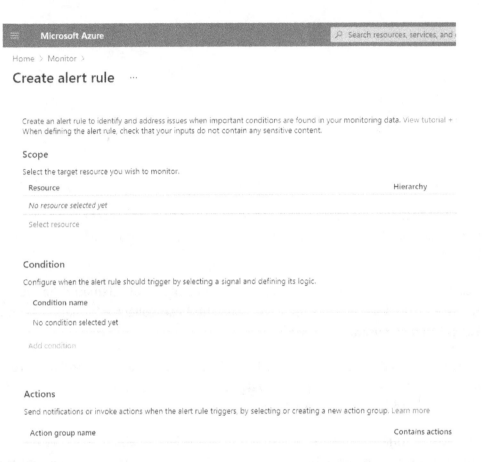

Azure Monitor is accessed from your Azure Portal.

Within Azure Monitor, you can also write custom queries for the data stored in Azure Log Analytics. These queries are written in a SQL-like language called KQL (Kusto Query Language).

```
SQLDBEvents
| where EventType == 'Logon' and StartTime > datetime(2020-01-01)
| count
```

GitHub

GitHub is another cloud-hosted implementation of Git. It does have an on-premises GitHub Enterprise version but that is not of interest to me in my analytic work.

There is a common misconception that GitHub is only used for public repositories and open-source code. GitHub supports both public and private repositories.

GitHub is so widely used that it now holds most code being developed world-wide. A few years back, Microsoft purchased GitHub and has been starting to integrate it into their offerings, and, with Azure DevOps.

Azure DevOps Concept	GitHub Concept
Organization	Organization (but also Enterprise)
Project	N/A
Repos	Repository
Pipelines	Workflows/Actions
Boards	Issues

In the table above, I have provided a rough mapping of GitHub concepts with the Azure DevOps concepts that I have already described.

Project really does not have an equivalent.

Workflows and Actions are becoming more capable. The continuous integration aspects are quite equivalent to what you can do in a build pipeline in Azure DevOps. The continuous deployment aspects though are poor, when compared to Azure DevOps, at least at the time of writing.

Issues also is currently a long way short of the capabilities of Azure Boards.

If you are keen to use GitHub as it has much of your other code, note that you can use GitHub as a repository directly from within Azure DevOps.

GitHub vs Azure DevOps

Today, for most of my clients, I would choose Azure DevOps every time. GitHub is the long-term stated directly for Microsoft, but Azure DevOps is not disappearing any time soon. Microsoft themselves have a hug investment in it with their own code.

I think Azure DevOps currently offers a better starting point for learning about DevOps, and it has a better initial story where you can have up to five users for free. This can let your team get proficiency at low cost. Azure DevOps also has much richer overall functionality, and costs less than GitHub. (Note: this might change in time)

Another issue that might affect your decision about which tool to use is YAML. (Yet another markup language). In Azure DevOps, "classic" pipelines are constructed using a graphical user interface that will be familiar to any Windows user. In recent years, there has been a choice to create pipelines in YAML instead. I find that most of my clients still prefer the graphical interface, rather than a page of text that is highly dependent upon things like indentation.

In GitHub, Actions are defined using YAML. There is no graphical equivalent. I have found that when clients are coming from other tools like Terraform, etc. that use YAML, they naturally adapt to YAML in either GitHub Actions or YAML pipelines in Azure DevOps. However, clients without this type of background, tend to prefer the graphical options in Azure DevOps.

Database Projects

When I create an Azure DevOps project, I typically create three repositories:

- Database project repository for each database

- Azure Data Factory (ADF) repository for each data factory

- Tabular data model project

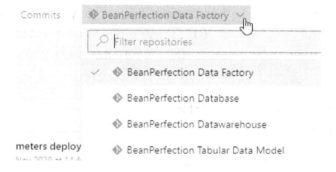

For the database projects, there are two ways that I might create the projects. They differ based upon how the code will be deployed.

The most common method is to use a SQL Server Database Project as part of SQL Server Data Tools (SSDT). If I have an existing database, I can create a project then immediately import the existing code from the database. Alternately, I can start from scratch with the project.

I have many standard scripts like those for creating my normal schemas, etc. that I will bring into the project.

When you use database projects in SSDT, you modify the code in the project and then build the project to create a DACPAC as the output. The DACPAC can then be deployed to the target server.

A less common method is that I will use a repository to just store a series of SQL scripts that have been used to create the database, but they will not be part of a database project. I generally only do this for client teams that are not mature in their development practices.

I prefer deploying directly from the database projects in SSDT however, as you then are sure that what is in the target database matches what is in source control. Far too often I see situations where clients have database scripts in source control, yet they do not match the code that is deployed.

Database Projects in SSDT

Database projects were added as a new type of project template in Visual Studio many years ago. You do not need to already have a Visual Studio license to use them, and they are free for developers to use. Up to Visual Studio 2017, these projects were available with a standalone installer. From Visual Studio 2019 onwards, they were added as standard extensions to Visual Studio.

There are options for how the files and folders will be laid out. You can import a database's contents, and you can also import SQL scripts.

I generally use the default folder structure where Schemas are the top-level items, and Functions, Stored Procedures, Tables, Views, etc. are sub-folders.

In a database project, each object is represented by a separate file. This makes it easy to compare project in source control, and changes across versions.

Building a Database Project

You can use any .NET build template to start working with building a database project from within Azure DevOps. Generally, I remove any steps except ones that build the solution, that copy the output files to the staging areas, and then publish the artifacts.

When you run the build pipeline, the output is a DACPAC file. DACPAC files contain just schema and metadata. They do not contain any user data. There is an alternate type of file that can contain data. It is called a BACPAC file. Each of these files is a .zip file. A DACPAC file just has a .dacpac extension, but if you rename a DACPAC file to a .zip file, you will be able to see its contents.

A DACPAC file represents the desired state for the database. The deployment tooling then attempts to make the target database match the defined structure within the DACPAC file.

Under the covers, the key tool that is used is called SQLPackage. If you review the documentation for sqlpackage.exe, you will see the wide variety of options that it provides, that can let you closely control how the deployment will occur.

Change Management Advice

I will close this chapter with some advice on working with database projects. Try to follow this advice:

- Keep changes small

- Deploy changes regularly (do not build up a big list of changes)

- Avoid adding and deleting objects in the same deployment

- Avoid messy changes completely (e.g., changing a column's data type)

Chapter 8: Staging, Loading and Transforming Data

Overview

In this chapter I will cover how I get data into the DataModel tables.

I will describe how I access source system data, how I create our Staging and DataLoad schemas, and how I then load the staged data.

Awesome image by Milivoj Kuhar

Accessing Source Data

Source data will be found in a variety of locations. When I am implementing these projects, the first thing I aim to do, is to get the data into the cloud (usually Azure). Most times I want to stage the data into an Azure SQL Database.

Data from any type of SQL server will be copied directly into staging tables in my data warehouse database. Data that is contained in files will be first copied into an Azure storage account, then later copied into the staging tables in the data warehouse database.

What I do: File Processing

Most of the time, I am dealing with csv or tsv files, but occasionally XML files or other formats. I will do an initial staging of the files into Azure storage with the following structure:

- A container for the project (e.g., salesanalysis)

- A staging folder for files that are not processed yet (e.g., salesanalysis/staging)

- An archive folder for files that have been processed (e.g., salesanalysis/archive)

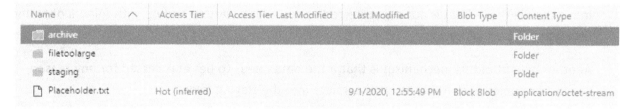

Name	Access Tier	Access Tier Last Modified	Last Modified	Blob Type	Content Type
archive					Folder
filetoolarge					Folder
staging					Folder
Placeholder.txt	Hot (inferred)		9/1/2020, 12:55:49 PM	Block Blob	application/octet-stream

Note that in the example above, I also have a folder for "filetoolarge". This was a special situation for this project. I almost always use Azure Data Factory (ADF) to orchestrate the moving of the files. The typical logic flow will be:

- Copy any source files that need processing into the staging folder

- Process all files in the staging folder (generally by executing a stored procedure in the data warehouse database)

- Move each file to the archive folder as it is processed.

I do it this way to allow for any situation where processing of a file fails, or if the process is interrupted for any reason. If the processing of a file fails or is interrupted, it will stay in the staging folder and be processed again the next time the import pipeline runs.

I design the processing phase so that it is idempotent whenever I can. That means that no matter how many times I reprocess the same file, the same outcome is achieved. Data is not duplicated or missed.

If a file fails, I leave it in the staging folder and flag an error on the pipeline so it will be investigated, corrected, and reprocessed. One alternative to this, is to have another folder for faulty files and move the file there. That is not my preferred option as it is easy to end up with folders of faulty files that no-one looks at.

Another benefit of this mechanism is that if the data needs to be reprocessed for any reason, it can just be copied back from the archive folder into the staging folder.

What I do: Database Data

Ideally, the source data that I work with would already be in an Azure SQL database. If that is not the case, my first step is to try to get it into one of these databases first. Generally, if I am working with data from an on-premises SQL Server database, I will create a replica in Azure. Importantly, it will usually only be a subset the source data: a subset of tables, and potentially even a subset of columns in the tables.

To push data into that replica, I use one of five methods, in order of preference:

- SQL Data Sync (least preferred method)

- Integration Services package (reasonable method)

- Linked server and custom SQL Server Agent job (reasonable method)

- Availability Group Replica (reasonable method)

- Transactional Replication (most preferred method)

Transactional Replication

If you have not worked with transactional replication before, it works on a publisher/distributor/subscriber metaphor, modeled on a magazine distribution business.

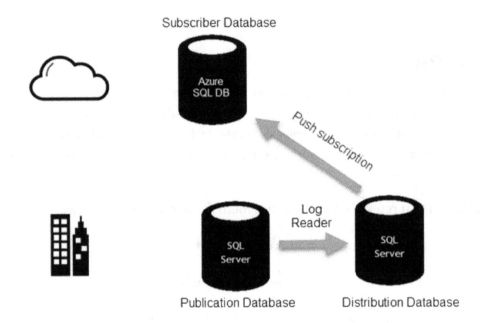

The steps are as follows:

- A source database is the publisher.

- A log reader agent extracts data changes from the database log. This is important because it has minimal impact on the source system's performance.

- The changes are written to a distribution database. This holds changes for as long as they are needed by subscribers.

- The changes are copied from the distribution database to any subscribers in either a "push" or "pull" method. For push, the agent on the distributor pushes the changes to the subscriber. In pull, the agent on the subscriber pulls the changes from the distributor.

With data moving from on-premises SQL Server to an Azure SQL database, we use a push subscription, and it runs continuously. Within seconds, changes that occur on-premises end up in the subscription tables in the Azure SQL database.

Transactional Replication Pros and Cons

Transactional replication is very useful because all the hard work is done by the framework provided:

- The data is updated constantly and with relatively low latency

- There is minimal latency (updates appear in the cloud quite quickly)

- There is a reasonable tolerance for schema changes at the source (This was not always the case)

- The subscriber can be set up quite differently to the source system.

The subscriber does not have to be a direct copy of how the source is configured. For example, you can adjust data types, and the table structures. One common example is that you might have an IDENTITY column at the source, but you do not want it to be an IDENTITY column in the replica. Instead, it can just be an int or bigint data type. Similarly, a rowversion (or timestamp) column at the source, might need to be a binary value at the subscriber.

You can also have a different indexing strategy. This is useful because you might need different indexes to support your analytic queries, but you cannot add them to the source system either. If they were added to the source, they would slow it down too much. The vendor might also not allow those types of changes.

There are downsides to Transactional Replication though.

It had a reputation in the past for being difficult to set up and to manage. Much of that reputation came from Merge Replication which I never use. By comparison, Transactional Replication is now very easy to work with. I have many customers using it to replicate data from on-premises SQL Server systems to Azure SQL databases. It is easy to set up and it generally just keeps working well.

There is a learning curve if you want to be proficient with it. If you need help with it, we have an online course at our site: https://training.sqldownunder.com.

Not all source systems can be replicated. Third party application vendors might not allow you to replicate their databases. Some of these vendors also make database changes that are not friendly to any type of downstream system. I see some vendors who just suddenly change the data type of a column, or others who, when they want to change a reference table, just drop the table, and recreate it, rather than altering it. As another example of a bizarre source system, I came across a vendor who had aliased the smalldatetime data type as "date". This means that they had a "date" data type, but it was not actually a date data type. You just cannot allow for all the odd things that vendors might do. Bizarre source systems will require custom analytic staging designs.

Common Data Flow

When I am using transactional replication, the most common data flow is as follows:

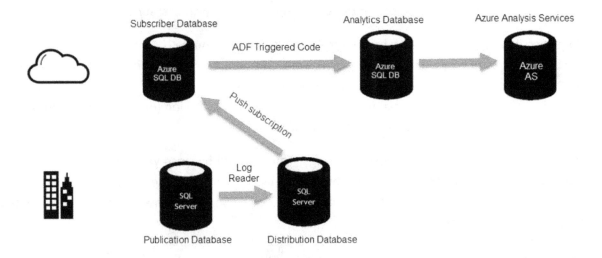

The source data is published, and changes are read into the Distribution database. Those changes are then pushed into the Subscriber database in Azure. Azure Data Factory periodically runs queries to put the required data into the data warehouse database (shown in the figure as the Analytics database), and the data is finally loaded into Analysis Services or Power BI Premium.

Linked server and custom SQL Server Agent job

While transactional replication can do most of the hard work for you, it cannot always be used. In those situations, we often do the following:

- Create a linked server (from the on-premises SQL Server to the Azure SQL database)

- Create a stored procedure that runs on the on-premises system that moves and synchronizes the data between the on-premises database and the cloud database

- Create a SQL Server Agent job to periodically execute the stored procedure.

Integration Services Package

One other option with on-premises SQL Server is to create an Integration Services package that connects to both the on-premises and cloud databases and performs the required synchronization. This is more work to set up but can be a useful method if other options fail.

It might also be a preferred option if the team that is implementing the project has more experience with Integration Services than with the required T-SQL for a custom stored procedure.

Availability Group Replica

One final option that I will mention is to have an Availability Group replica in Azure.

In larger enterprises who are using availability groups on-premises, it might be possible to set up an asynchronous readable replica in Azure. It would need to be asynchronous as a synchronous replica would introduce far too much latency on the primary replica. For analytics though, this would work well. The data would be nearly up to date constantly, and readable as a source of analytic data.

This option requires higher level database management skills to work with, but my greatest concern is that setting it up, just to provide analytic data, would likely be cost-prohibitive.

Creating the Staging Schema

Staging Schema in the Data Warehouse Structure

I use the Staging schema as a landing point for data. Importantly, I bring the data into this schema prior to performing any substantial transformation. Failure often occurs when data is being transformed. I want the process of staging the data to succeed as often as possible. Keeping the transformation work till later helps to ensure this.

As a reminder, this is where the Staging schema fits into the plan:

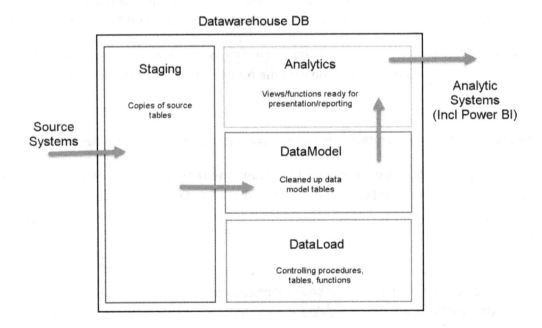

What I do: Staging Schema

The Staging schema is where source data lands.

- Whenever possible, I try to keep the same table and column names that are present in the source.

- I only import columns that are useful

- I generally use the same data types as the source system.

- I generally make all the columns NULLable

- ⊟ ▦ Staging.tblBCatSpPr
  - ⊟ ▦ Columns
    - ⟜ recid (PK, int, not null)
    - ⊟ bus_cat_code (varchar(8), no
    - ⊟ stock_code (varchar(8), not
    - ⊟ discpercent (decimal(18,3),
    - ⊟ discdollars (decimal(18,2),
    - ⊟ established (datetime, not n
    - ⊟ cost (decimal(18,2), not nul
    - ⊟ overrideprice (smallint, not
    - ⊟ promo_from (datetime, not nu
    - ⊟ promo_to (datetime, not null
  - ⊞ ▦ Keys
  - ⊞ ▦ Constraints
  - ⊞ ▦ Triggers
  - ⊞ ▦ Indexes
  - ⊞ ▦ Statistics
- ⊞ ▦ Staging.tblBGrp
- ⊞ ▦ Staging.tblBGrpSpPr
- ⊞ ▦ Staging.tblBusCat
- ⊞ ▦ Staging.tblContGnrl
- ⊞ ▦ Staging.tblContSpPr
- ⊞ ▦ Staging.tblContTran
- ⊞ ▦ Staging.tblCustBOrd
- ⊞ ▦ Staging.tblCustInvL
- ⊞ ▦ Staging.tblCustInvo
- ⊞ ▦ Staging.tblCustOrdL
- ⊞ ▦ Staging.tblCustOrdr
- ⊞ ▦ Staging.tblPkg
- ⊞ ▦ Staging.tblStkCat
- ⊞ ▦ Staging.tblStokGnrl

The exception to using the same data types as the source is that I will not build my Staging schema tables with deprecated data types:

- If the source is a text column, I will use varchar(max)

- If the source is an ntext column, I will use nvarchar(max)

- If the source is an image column, I will use varbinary(max)

It is important not to use the deprecated data types in any new work, including here in the Staging schema.

The data in the Staging schema tables is not retained long-term. It is only kept during the loading process. The DataModel tables are used for the longer-term storage. The Staging schema tables are usually truncated prior to each staging operation.

NULL or NOT NULL

To avoid any loading issues, and to help allow for changes in the source system, I will often make all the Staging schema columns NULL rather than copying the NULL or NOT NULL settings from the source. If there is value in keeping the NOT NULL options, I consider keeping them. The example in the figure above shows an example where I retained them.

Generally, I configure them all as NULL. This is just to protect my data warehouse from changes in the source system. If the source database has a column that is defined as NOT NULL, and I use NOT NULL in my Staging schema tables, a problem might arise if the source system table gets redefined as NULL. Next time I bring data in, I might get a NULL value and then my import process is going to fail, really for no great reason.

Using External Tables to Access Source Data

If the data being loaded into the Staging schema is from an Azure SQL database, I use external tables to make the connection. If you have worked with linked servers in the past, the concept is similar, except that it based at the table level and is far more flexible.

To access one Azure SQL database from another, there are three steps:

- Create a database scoped credential

- Create an external data source

- Create the required external tables

The first object required is a database scoped credential. This is basically just a name given to a username and password. I need a credential that can be used to log onto the other database.

The second object required is an external data source. You can think of this as a name given to a set of connection details for another server and database.

Once I have created the external data source, it appears in Object Explorer in SQL Server Management Studio under the External Resources node:

```
⊟ ▣ External Resources
   ⊟ ▣ External Data Sources
        ▣ AquSell_DatabaseServer
```

The external data source is configured to use the database scoped credential when logging on.

The final objects needed are external tables. They are local metadata for remote tables. You can think of these as views over the remote tables or views.

Like a view, they do not hold any data. External tables appear in Object Explorer under the Tables node:

```
⊟ ▦ Tables
   ⊞ ▦ System Tables
   ⊟ ▦ External Tables
      ⊞ 🗊 AquSell.tblBCatSpPr
      ⊞ 🗊 AquSell.tblBGrp
      ⊞ 🗊 AquSell.tblBGrpSpPr
      ⊞ 🗊 AquSell.tblBusCat
      ⊞ 🗊 AquSell.tblContGnrl
```

There are two things that I commonly do when naming these tables:

- I create a schema for the remote data source (in this example, it was AquSell)

- I create the tables with the same names they have in the source

Once this is set up, I can read from these tables in my queries, the same way that I can read from other local tables within the database.

What I do: Linked Servers

If you are working with on-premises servers and need to use linked servers, there are just a few issues that I need to point out.

The most common misconfiguration that I see with linked servers is the "Collation Compatible" setting. I cannot stress how important this setting is. The setting tells SQL Server if it can trust the sorting at the remote server. Imaging I have a query that finds a customer with a name of Terry. If my server trusts the remote server's sorting, it can send a query that just retrieves the row for Terry. However, if my server does not trust the remote server to correctly resolve the collation, it needs to return **every** row from the remote table and filter than locally. You can imagine the difference in performance.

A second issue is that you should avoid putting the name of the linked server in your code. Do not write queries that access tables like **SomeServer.SomeDatabase.SomeSchema.SomeTable**. While this works, it introduces a major maintenance issue.

Instead, create a synonym for each table on the linked server and use that synonym throughout your code. Then when the linked server name changes, you only need to update the synonyms.

Indexing Staged Tables

While the tables in the Staging schema are copies or subsets of source tables, you do not need to have the same indexing that the source system uses. The indexing for those tables needs to reflect what is needed by the queries that will be run against the staged data, now how it was processed in the source system.

As you develop the queries for processing the staged data, you should ensure that appropriate indexes exist to support those queries.

Creating the DataLoad Schema

DataLoad Schema in the Data Warehouse Structure

I need to store data that controls the loading processes, and the procedures that perform the processing. I use the DataLoad schema for this.

As a reminder, this is where the DataLoad schema fits into the plan:

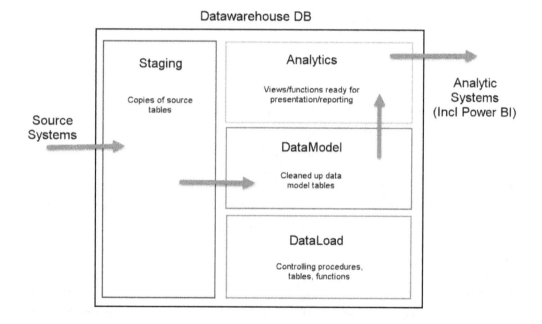

What I do: DataLoad Schema

The DataLoad schema does not hold any user data. Instead, it holds:

- Integration-related objects

- Functions and procedures used for data loading

- Configuration data

- Logging data

```
⊟ 📇 Stored Procedures
  ⊞ 📇 System Stored Procedures
  ⊞ 📄 DataLoad.GetRecentLogEntries
  ⊞ 📄 DataLoad.RefreshExternalAndStagingObjects
  ⊞ 📄 DataLoad.StageSourceSystemData
  ⊞ 📄 DataLoad.WriteLogEntry
```

Any tables in this schema are only required for controlling the loading process. Mostly, that will involve recording where an integration process is up to. For example, I might need to store the last ID value of a table that is being loaded incrementally.

In some systems, I will also have mapping tables in this schema if they are not required in the DataModel schema. Even though I try to avoid it due to the future maintenance overhead, at times, you need to have a table that maps values from one system to another.

What I do: Automation Metadata

There is an old saying that whenever possible, you should aim to write code that writes code, instead of just writing code. When you find yourself writing a lot of boiler-plate code (very repetitive code), you should consider automating the process instead.

As an example, rather than creating external data sources, external tables, staging tables, indexes, loading queries, etc. all manually, I try to automate the process. Instead of creating the objects, I add what is required as rows in metadata tables, and I then write code that will auto-generate all the required objects and procedures automatically.

160

The tables and procedures that I use for this, are also placed in the DataLoad schema:

⊞ ▦ DataLoad.ExternalTables
⊞ ▦ DataLoad.LoadingQueries
⊞ ▦ DataLoad.LogEntries
⊞ ▦ DataLoad.StagingIndexes
⊞ ▦ DataLoad.SystemConfiguration

This type of automation is beyond the scope of this book, but I encourage you to explore it.

Loading File Data into Staging Tables

Where I have pre-staged file data in Azure storage account folders, I try to read the file data directly into the Staging schema tables.

With CSV or TSV data, I use the T-SQL OPENROWSET command to read the Azure data. For XML data, I use the T-SQL XML query options. Generally this involves pulling the XML from the blob storage into a T-SQL variable and then querying the variable using the .query() and .nodes() methods.

What I do: Logging

In the DataLoad schema, I also add the following:

- A table to hold events related to staging and loading data

- A logging stored procedure that writes details of these events

- A procedure to retrieve staging and loading events

I call the logging stored procedure from within all the other procedures that are involved in staging or loading of data.

Loading Staged Data

Incremental Data Loading

Whenever possible, I try to perform incremental loading of data to avoid the overhead of reloading entire sets of data. The larger the source data tables are, the more important it will be to load data from them incrementally.

Tables in the DataLoad schema can be used to hold ID values that indicate where the incremental loading process is up to.

Not all tables can be incrementally loaded. The common methods are:

- Auto-increment values. If the table has an auto-increment value like an IDENTITY column, this might be able to be used for incremental loading.

- DateTime values. The data might include a datetime value that can be used to find rows that need to be copied.

- LastModified values. The row might include a value that indicates when it was last modified. Be very careful with these values though and check how they get set. They often are not reliable.

It is important to check though, if previously loaded rows can later be modified. If so, an overlapping scheme or a full load scheme would be needed.

Loading and Transforming the Staged Data

The final step is that the data that has been staged needs to be transformed and loaded into the DataModel tables.

I usually do this by executing a stored procedure that is held in the DataLoad schema. Transformations that are required will be performed in the T-SQL code. SQL is very efficient at performing the transformations. The procedure will have a name like LoadStagedXXXX.

If a full reload of the table is needed, the procedure will first truncate the DataModel table.

I also try to make these procedures idempotent. I try to design them so that they can be run more than once, and still have the same outcome, without duplicating or missing data.

Chapter 9: Implementing ELT and Processing

Overview

The next thing I want to discuss is the ELT process. In the industry, we used to talk about ETL processes (extract, transform, load) but it is generally accepted nowadays that extracting data, loading it, and then transforming it, almost always leads to a better outcome.

I will discuss the tooling that I use for this processing, and then introduce Azure Data Factory (ADF) where we orchestrate the end-to-end data movement.

ADF has a few tricks around triggers and scheduling, so I will cover those. I will show you how we work with security and identity in ADF, and finally, I will show you how it integrates with source control and deployment.

Awesome image by Steven Ramon

ELT Tooling

The way that I orchestrate the data movement and transformation is dependent upon whether that data movement is happening on-premises or in Azure.

What I do: On-Premises

For on-premises work, I use SQL Server Integration Services (SSIS). It is a very mature and capable integration tool.

I create packages that do the work. Note that I try to avoid row-by-row data transformation in SSIS. While the tool is very capable of performing that transformation, doing so is highly inefficient when compared to performing the same transformations in SQL.

SSIS packages also make it very easy to work with Analysis Services either in Azure or on-premises.

If you need training on SSIS, we have a dedicated course here:
https://training.sqldownunder.com.

Once I have created the required packages, I schedule them in one of two ways:

- SQL Server Agent can easily schedule SSIS packages, and can control the identity used for executing the packages

- Some organizations have enterprise schedulers (like Control-M). These are used to schedule everything happening in the enterprise. Importantly, they also capture all the logging output and bring it back to a central location. That can greatly improve manageability of the tasks being scheduled.

What I do: Azure

When developers who used to work with SSIS, started moving their systems to the cloud, they were asking "Where is my cloud-based SSIS?". The answer to that question was that they should use Azure Data Factory (ADF) instead, but it is important to understand that ADF is not "SSIS in the cloud".

When I need to orchestrate data integration in the Azure, I use ADF. Instead of packages in SSIS, it has a concept of pipelines and I use them for:

- Moving or copying or migrating source database data

- Moving or copying files

- Processing Azure Analysis Services data models

The scheduling of the pipelines is performed by ADF triggers. There are several types of triggers, and I will introduce ADF and these triggers next.

Azure Data Factory (ADF) Overview

ADF is a hybrid data integration service. Even though it is cloud-based, it can reach down and work with on-premises systems as well by using locally-installed integration runtimes.

ADF is a fully managed Platform as a Service (PaaS) offering. It is designed to let you build integration projects in a low-code manner. In fact, a great deal of work can be done with almost no code. The only code I tend to write in ADF is when I need to use its expression language. (And yes, it has its own unique expression language).

Microsoft build ADF on top of Data Bricks. When you interact with the designer UI, you are visually creating objects that are transformed into the Scala language and deployed to Data Bricks clusters. Each object that you are building can be represented as a JSON object. This is important as it lets ADF work well with source code control systems Git-based systems.

Early versions of ADF had an option to build projects in Visual Studio. That option is no longer present. All development happens in the designer UI.

Keep in mind that in the description of ADF that follows that the UI is constantly evolving. I wish I could promise you that you will find settings in the same place that I have shown them but that would be a false promise. Generally, though, the concept is the same even if the location moves.

SSIS Packages in ADF

It is possible to migrate SSIS packages directly into ADF and run them on a special SSIS integration runtime. I see Microsoft staff pushing this regularly. I can only assume they see it as a low-friction way to move packages to the cloud.

I almost never do this.

I have a strong preference for using native ADF code. For most clients, native code will be beneficial to them in the future.

However, there is one scenario where I would consider using SSIS packages directly in ADF, and that is where the client has many complex packages and there simply is not time or budget to refactor them to work natively in ADF.

167

ADF Project Structure

The first object that you create when working with ADF is the data factory itself. I am often asked about how to structure projects when using ADF. With SSIS, in Visual Studio, you could have one solution and many SSIS projects within the solution. Each project could also have many packages.

Do not make the mistake of trying to minimize the number of data factories that you use. I see users thinking that they will create one data factory and create all the pipelines that they need within that one data factory. It is not like creating a database server and having a number of databases on it.

Instead, think of a data factory as a folder, holding a collection of pipelines, and the other objects that those pipelines need. Importantly, the data factory gets deployed, not the individual pipelines. Deploying individual pipelines is possible but it is not how ADF works by default.

So, try to only group related pipelines into a single data factory. Be prepared to have many data factories. And for each data factory that you use in development, you might have other data factories in other environments like testing, UAT, production, etc. You do not pay for having individual data factories, only for executing pipelines (or SSIS integration runtimes) in those data factories.

The following figure shows part of the home page in the Azure portal for my BeanPerfectionDataFactory:

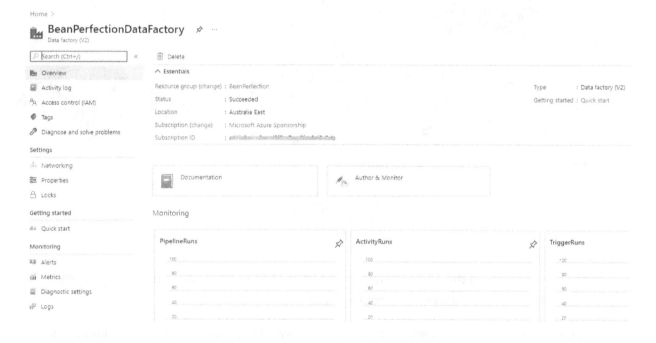

The most important link on this home page is the one that says, "Author & Monitor". That opens the ADF designer:

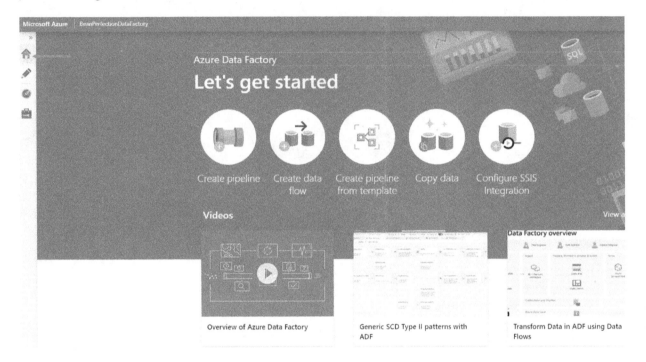

Instead of entering via the Azure portal, I could have opened adf.azure.com and logged on there instead. I almost always enter from the Azure portal.

This home page is not useful once you are familiar with the product. It has a few links to videos and tutorials. Previously it had links to source control, etc. but they have all moved elsewhere now. This is the same page that you would be returned to if you clicked the **Home** icon in the left-hand pane.

Creating ADF Pipelines

The **Author** icon in the left-hand pane is where the editing begins.

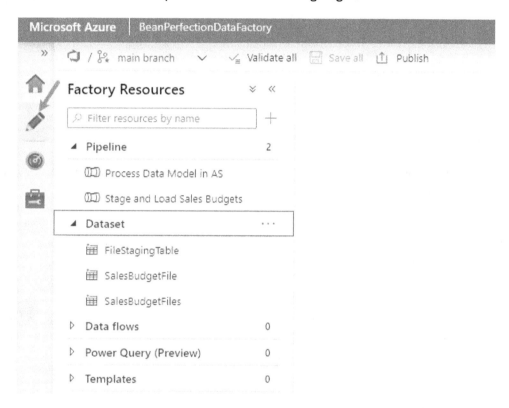

In the above image, I have clicked the **Author** icon to enter the editing mode. I have then expanded my list of pipelines, and my list of datasets.

If I click on the second pipeline, I see this:

This is the area where you can edit a pipeline. If you have worked with SSIS before, many aspects of this will be familiar.

Each pipeline has a set of general properties. You can see these by clicking in the whitespace in the pipeline editor and then clicking the icon near the top right of the screen:

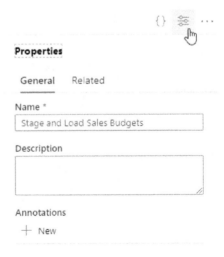

At the bottom of the screen, you can also then see also see other settings:

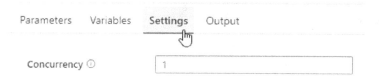

I have highlighted the Settings tab here to show the Concurrency setting. This indicates how many copies of the same pipeline can run at the same time. I have chosen to limit it to a single concurrent execution.

Activities

The boxes that are connected in the pipeline are called Activities (like Tasks in the Control Flow for SSIS readers). The center pane offers a list of activities that you can select:

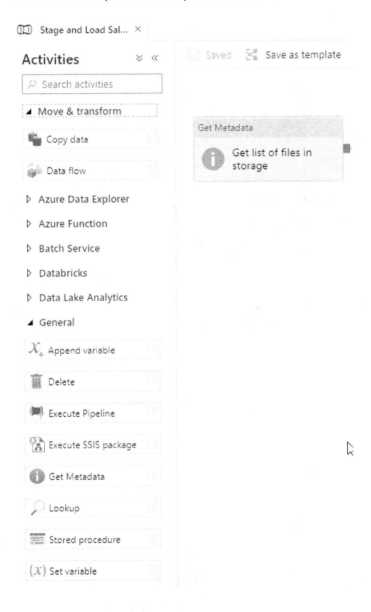

There is a reasonably rich set of activities available, and the list of activities is being added to over time. ADF is being developed constantly.

Activities can be dragged out onto the pipeline editor and can be connected to each other by using dependencies.

When you click on an activity, a new set of icons appears on the activity:

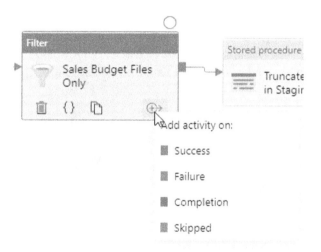

The default type of dependency is Success. You can add dependency types by clicking on the plus sign in the circle with the arrow as shown above.

One glaring limitation of ADF today is that if you have two dependencies leading to an activity, they are treated as an AND combination. In SSIS, we could create OR relationships for precedence constraints. That is not possible in ADF at present. I hope that will be rectified soon.

If you are used to working with SSIS, you might also be surprised that you cannot disable an activity (skip over it) or execute an individual activity. I hope these abilities are added in the future.

The other three icons that appear in the image above are:

- Trash can – is used to delete the activity

- Curly braces – is used to see the JSON representation of the activity (It is also possible to edit that manually)

- Two sheets – is used to clone the activity.

Also notice the red circle that has appeared above the activity. If you click on it, and it turns solid red, then this activity will have a breakpoint. Execution will stop after this activity has completed.

Another thing that changes when I click on the activity is that its property pane appears below:

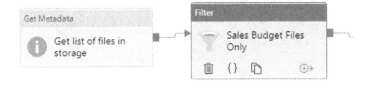

General   Settings   User properties

Name * | Sales Budget Files Only | Learn r

Description | |
                       | |

176

If I click on the curly braces on an activity, I see the associated JSON:

```json
{
    "name": "Sales Budget Files Only",
    "type": "Filter",
    "dependsOn": [
      {
          "activity": "Get list of files in storage",
          "dependencyConditions": [
            "Succeeded"
          ]
      }
    ],
    "userProperties": [],
    "typeProperties": {
      "items": {
          "value": "@activity('Get list of files in storage').output.childItems",
          "type": "Expression"
      },
      "condition": {
          "value": "@and(startsWith(item().name, 'sales'),endsWith(item().name, 'csv'))",
          "type": "Expression"
      }
    }
}
```

You can ignore the JSON while doing most editing in ADF, but it is important to know that when you are using the UI, that is what you are creating under the covers.

Pipeline Parameters

Another tab on the properties of a pipeline allows you to configure parameters. These are inbound parameters. You will often use them to provide specific configuration to an execution of a pipeline. For example, I have recently been working with timber mills, and while I might run a pipeline for each mill, it will be the same pipeline, and it will have a parameter to say which mill needs to be processed.

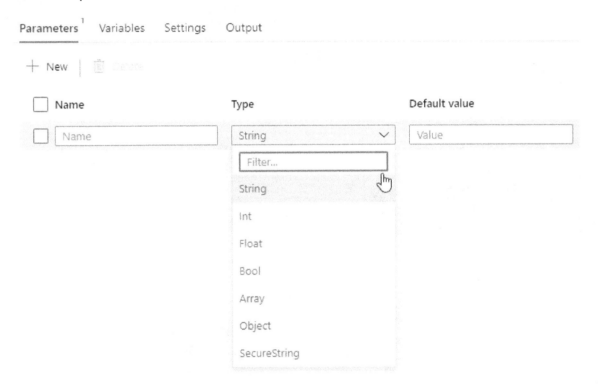

When I started working with ADF, one thing that really surprised me was the list of data types that I could use for parameters. Note that it is quite a limited list of types.

For each parameter, you can also set a default value. This will be used if the value is NULL at runtime. It is also very helpful to avoid you needing to constantly enter parameter values while you are developing pipelines.

Pipeline Variables

Unlike pipeline parameters that are inbound, pipeline variables can be used to read and write values throughout the execution of a pipeline.

In the image above, you are seeing the entire list of data types that can be used for variables. I really found this hard to believe when I started working with ADF. Notice that there is not even a single numeric data type. I wish this list had more data types as it makes coding expressions more difficult than it needs to be.

Linked Services

ADF is most used to move data and/or files around. That requires connections to databases, storage account, and even to key vaults that hold the usernames and passwords that are required.

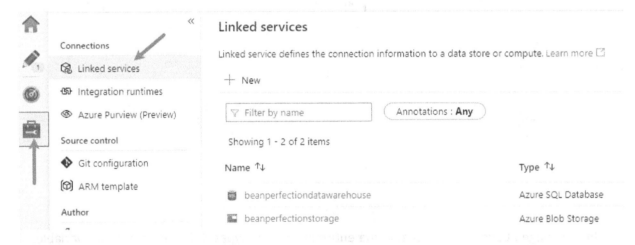

Linked services are accessed by clicking on the **Manage** icon (the toolkit) in the left-hand pane, then clicking on the **Linked services** list under **Connections**.

Data Sets

If you think of linked services as connections to the services, you can think of datasets as queries that are run against those services or database tables, or other objects located at those services.

In the image above, I have selected the FileStagingTable dataset to open its properties. Note that this dataset uses the beanperfectiondatawarehouse linked service. And rather than a query, I am connecting to a table.

The schema of the table is FileStaging, but the name of the table has been parameterized. This allows me to use the same dataset for many tables in the same schema. It avoids creating separate datasets for each table.

The "@dataset().TableName" value is an example of the ADF expression language. It is saying "the value of the TableName parameter in the current dataset".

NOTE: The expression language is case-sensitive. I wish it were not. I have a strong aversion to case-sensitivity in code. It really offers little advantages and has so many disadvantages and leads to so many errors.

You can see how that has been configured on the Parameters tab:

I could just as easily have configured the Schema Name as a parameter as well.

Timeouts

ADF supports timeouts on many activities. I think the default value for timeout is way too long. The default value is 7 days.

Instead, when I drag an activity out to the editor, the first property that I always set is the timeout value:

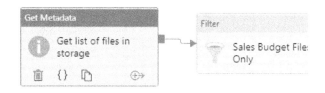

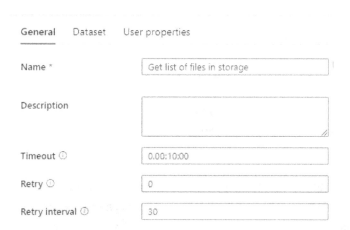

The value represents days, hours, minutes, and seconds.

In this same section, you can also decide if an activity should be retried when it fails, and if so, after what delay interval.

Integration Runtimes

Code, activities, and connections in ADF need to run somewhere. They run on an integration runtime (IR).

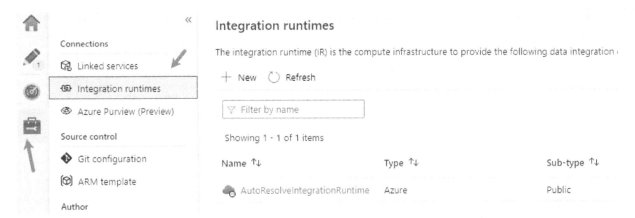

ADF has a built-in IR called AutoResolveIntegrationRuntime. This is all you need for many projects. It is a shared resource, but I have found it works well. You can create your own IR and specify the type of virtual machine that you want if you really need to manage the performance of the IR.

However, this IR is Azure-based and if you need to connect to an on-premises data source or one that is not visible to the public Internet, you will need a self-hosted IR. This is code that is installed on a server within your network.

IRs normally are tied to individual data factories, but you can also share them between data factories. At the data factory where the IR is shared, it is called a Shared Integration Runtime. At the data factory that shares the IR, it is called a Linked Shared Integration Runtime.

There is also a special type of IR for executing SSIS packages. I mentioned that I try to avoid the use of SSIS directly inside ADF but if you decide that it is for you, ensure that you manage the ongoing costs associated with the SSIS IR.

Testing Pipelines

When you have a pipeline ready to test, you can click the Debug option on the menu bar above the pipeline editor:

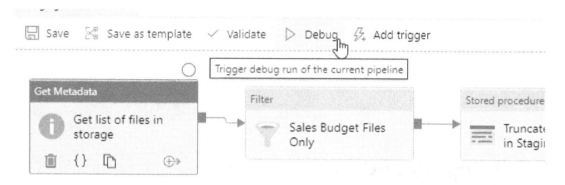

When you debug a pipeline, your code is loaded onto a debug Data Bricks cluster, not onto the cluster that you will use later when it is deployed and scheduled. At the bottom of the screen, you can see the progress as it continues.

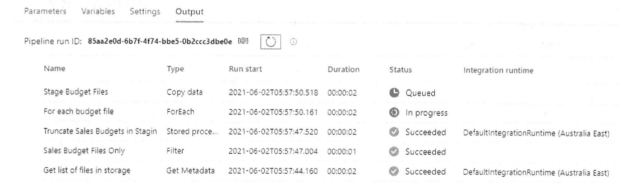

If an error occurs, you can click a link that is supplied to see the details of the error. If you hover over each activity, you can also see links that will show you any input or output to the activity.

ADF Triggers and Scheduling

Triggers are the mechanism used to execute pipelines automatically. There are several types of triggers that might be of interest.

Schedule Triggers

Schedule triggers are the most straightforward. They execute at a particular time and schedule. Not long ago, they could only be scheduled in UTC, but you can now schedule using your local time zone. That is important when you need to work with daylight savings time.

New trigger

Name *

Daily at 6_15AM and 10_15AM

Description

Type *

Schedule ⌄

Start date * ⓘ

06/02/2021 6:03 AM

Time zone * ⓘ

Canberra, Melbourne, Sydney (UTC+10) ⌄

Recurrence * ⓘ

Every 1   Day(s) ⌄

◢ Advanced recurrence options

Execute at these times   ⓘ

Hours   6 ✕ 10 ✕

Minutes   15 ✕

Schedule execution times
06:15,10:15

☐ Specify an end date

Annotations

+ New

Activated * ⓘ
◉ Yes ○ No

The default for schedule triggers is for every 15 minutes. If you change that setting to every 1 day, you get better configuration options for most scenarios. In the schedule above, I have configured the trigger to run at 6:15AM and 10:15AM. I name triggers for when they execute.

Triggers can be activated. That means they will execute. You can stop a trigger from firing by deactivating it.

You can manage all your triggers from the **Manage** tool, in the **Triggers** section:

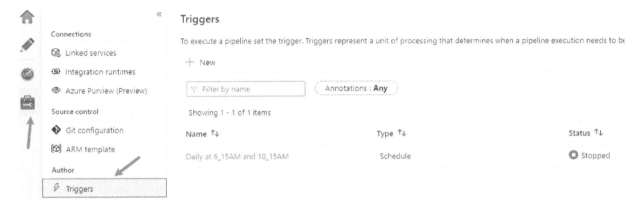

You can create a trigger in this same screen but be aware that ADF will not let you create an activated trigger unless is it associated with at least one pipeline. You can have a deactivated (stopped) trigger that is not associated with a pipeline.

Tumbling Window Triggers

These are an interesting type of trigger. They allow a trigger to fire after a specific period since the last time it fired. For example, I could execute a trigger every fifteen minutes.

The challenge with these triggers is that they have "memory". If I tell the trigger to start a year ago, and run every fifteen minutes, it will execute the pipeline for every fifteen-minute period since that year ago. And if I had not set the concurrency limit, I could end up with a very large number of pipelines running and queued.

Similarly, if I stop the trigger for two hours, when I restart it, it will again run for all the missing periods that it was stopped.

Tumbling window triggers are powerful but need careful design consideration.

Storage Event Triggers

These triggers are used to make a pipeline start when a file (or blob) is created or deleted in an Azure storage account.

Other Triggers

At the time of writing, there is another new type of trigger that is used for Custom Events. It is still in preview now. It allows you to track events from an Azure Event Grid topic.

Other Scheduling Methods

Because ADF has programmatic interfaces, it is also possible to schedule ADF pipeline executions by using external schedulers like enterprise schedulers.

ADF Security and Monitoring

Database and Service Connection Security

ADF often needs to connect to databases and might also need to connect to Analysis Services and Azure Key Vault. That requires ADF to use some type of identity when accessing the service.

For databases, it is common to store the required credentials in an Azure Key Vault. However, when you are using Azure SQL Database or Azure Analysis Services, there is another option to consider.

Back in the Azure portal home page for the data factory, there is a **Properties** tab:

⚙ **BeanPerfectionDataFactory** | Properties ⋯
Data factory (V2)

🔍 Search (Ctrl+/)	«
📊 Overview	
📝 Activity log	
👥 Access control (IAM)	
🏷 Tags	
🔧 Diagnose and solve problems	

Settings

🔀 Networking

⚙ Properties

🔒 Locks

Getting started

🚀 Quick start

Monitoring

🔔 Alerts

📊 Metrics

📈 Diagnostic settings

🔌 Logs

Automation

🔲 Tasks (preview)

Support + troubleshooting

Data factory
BeanPerfectionDataFactory

Location
australiaeast

Subscription
a⬛⬛⬛⬛⬛⬛⬛⬛⬛⬛⬛5db

Resource group
BeanPerfection

Provisioning state
Succeeded

Resource id
/subscriptions/a41fa⬛⬛⬛⬛⬛⬛⬛⬛⬛/resourceGroups/

Managed Identity Object ID
5625⬛⬛⬛⬛⬛⬛⬛⬛19f6

Managed Identity Tenant
cde8⬛⬛⬛⬛⬛⬛⬛7be19e

Managed Identity Application ID
376⬛⬛⬛⬛⬛⬛⬛387a

Each instance of ADF has a system-assigned identity. That identity can be used to connect to these services.

For example, when ADF needs to connect to an Azure Key Vault, the ADF can be assigned access policies to the key vault.

When ADF needs to connect to an Azure SQL Database, the identity of the ADF can be used to create a user in the database, and to assign permissions to it. To create any type of Azure AD user in Azure SQL Database, you need to be connected via an Azure AD based connection. While that sounds like a chicken and egg problem, you can configure an Azure AD Administrator for the database server, and use that user to create the other users required.

When ADF needs to connect to an Azure Analysis Services (AAS) server, the identity of the ADF can again be used, even as a service administrator. When configuring this on AAS, you need to specify the user as:

app:identity@tenant

You can get the identity value from the properties page above. It is listed as Managed Identity Application ID. You can also get the tenant value from the same screen. It is listed as Managed Identity Tenant.

Monitoring ADF and Creating Alerts

ADF has a built-in monitoring system. You can access it from the Monitoring icon in the left-hand pane in the editor.

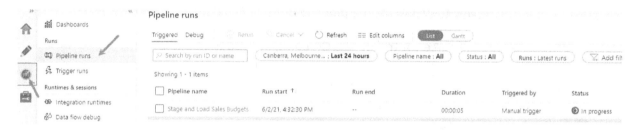

Both "triggered" and "debug" runs can be monitored. If you click onto a previous run, ADF opens the editor screen for that pipeline and shows you what occurred in each activity. This makes it very easy to work out what has happened.

If you want to be notified when an error occurs, you can also create an alert from within the same screen. I usually create at least one alert on the metric "failed pipeline runs" to let me know if any pipeline failed.

Integration with Source Control

It is important to integrate ADF with a Git-based source control. As mentioned earlier in this book, I tend to use Azure DevOps with Azure Repos for this.

If you do not have source control configured, you will find that you do not have Save buttons that you can use in the menus. The only option for you will be to Publish your data factory. The problem with that option is that you cannot publish a data factory that will not validate. So, if you are halfway through doing some work, you do not have an obvious way to save your work. (You can do it by manually saving the JSON for the pipeline but that is painful by comparison).

You can configure the source control on the **Git configuration** item in the **Manage** page:

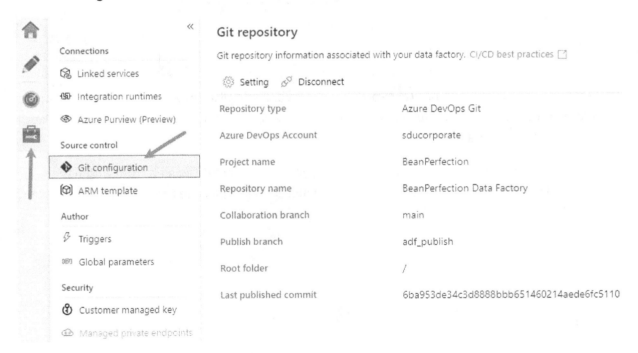

Once you have source control configured, when you start to work, you will be asked which branch you want to work in. By default, it will be the branch that you configured as the collaboration branch, but you can fork to create other branches.

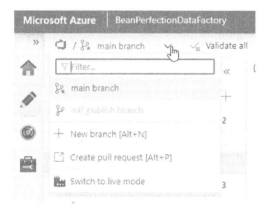

If you work in a separate (feature) branch, you can later create a pull request to merge the code back into the collaboration branch.

As soon as you have source control configured, you also then get workable Save buttons in the editor.

ADF does not provide an ability to compare code between commits or to merge code, but this is easily performed in your favorite source control tool.

ADF Deployment

You might then be wondering what happens when you click the Publish button.

This is used to create the ARM (Azure Resource Manager) templates that are used to deploy ADF using the default method. It first saves the work that you have been doing, and then converts all your JSON files into ARM template files. The ARM templates are placed into a separate adf_publish branch in the source repository.

The ARM templates are then published to your "real" data factory.

You can also build continuous deployment pipelines (using tools like Azure Pipelines) to deploy the templates.

I need to add a warning here.

If you ever use the standard ARM Template Deployment option in Azure Pipelines, make sure you always use the Incremental mode and never the Complete mode. If you use the Complete mode, you will replace your entire resource group with the data factory i.e., if your resource group had databases, storage accounts, etc., they will be gone. I wish that option had some red flashing lights around it.

Publishing from Code

Kamil Nowinski has created tooling that works with Azure Pipelines to make it much easier to deploy data factories. You can find his tools in the marketplace and find them online as "SQLPlayer". There is also a podcast at our sqldownunder.com where I discuss these tools with Kamil. I suggest listening to that podcast.

Kamil's tools allow you to exert fine control over the deployment, including deploying individual pipelines, and controlling the stopping and starting of triggers during deployment.

The ADF team has also recently been publishing some examples of how to deploy directly from code. I encourage you to consider these options rather than just using the ARM template-based deployment method.

ADF Data Flows

There is another core aspect of ADF that I have not discussed to this point in the book. There are two types of data flows that can be created:

- Data flows – these used to be called mapping data flows and basically just allow you to map data from the source to the sink (destination)

- Power Query flows – these used to be called wrangling data flows. These allow you to run Power Query queries to manipulate the data. You cannot do everything that you can do with Power Query elsewhere, but it is quite a good subset of capabilities.

I prefer not to do the heavy transformation work inside data flows, even though the Power Query story is compelling. Keep in mind that it was designed for power users and end users, and not for IT people.

There are many reasons why I would rather do transformation work in SQL rather than in Power Query. The first is that Power Query does not have strong data typing. Another is that the M language that Power Query uses is messy for many types of transformation. I recently saw a 50 step Power Query transformation that could have been a single SELECT query in SQL.

Chapter 10: Implementing the Tabular Model

Overview

In the next two chapters of this book, I will discuss how we work with tabular data models.

As I have mentioned previously, this could involve Azure Analysis Services, SQL Server Analysis Services, or Power BI Premium depending upon the client that we are working for and their cloud-tolerance that I discussed in the chapter on Power BI cloud implementation models.

Regardless of which target service we are using; we use the same tooling to build and deploy the projects: Visual Studio (SSDT) and Tabular Editor.

Awesome image by Victor Garcia

In this chapter I will also discuss how the tooling interacts with source control.

Structure and Tools

What I do: Tabular Data Model

The process that I use when creating tabular data models is to do the following:

- Import the Analytics views

- Create hierarchies

- Create common measures

- Hide key columns

- Set column summarization

- Configure the Date table

- Set column formatting

- Set column sort orders

- Set column categories

- Add an empty table as an anchor point for report-specific measures

- Implement row level security

I will explore each of these areas in this chapter.

What I do: Power BI

When I am consuming the tabular data model in Power BI, I do the following:

- Use a live connection to Analysis Services (if using a model in AS) or use a connection to a dataset (if in Power BI Premium)

- Add report-specific measures

- Design the visualizations

- Use workspaces for both logical groupings and for deployment environments

In will explore these areas in the final chapter.

What I do: Tooling

The tooling that I use for creating the tabular data models depends upon the type of customer that I am working with, as I described in the chapter on cloud implementation models.

SQL Server Analysis Services (SSAS)

If I am working with a cloud-conservative customer who wants to keep their data on-premises, then I work with SSAS. It is licensed with SQL Server and offers two editions that are of interest.

- Standard Edition

- Enterprise Edition

The main limitations that you get by using Standard Edition are:

- Your data model cannot contain perspectives

- Your data model cannot work with partitions (at least not as I would want to)

- You are limited to 128GB of memory (at the time of writing)

Azure Analysis Services (AAS) or Power BI Premium (PBI-P)

If I am working with a cloud-friendly customer, I will build their tabular data model in either AAS or in PBI-P.

AAS is a fully managed PaaS offering that you can rapidly deploy, and that is easy to manage. Often once I set it up, I barely think about it again. It just tends to keep on working. AAS is offered in two tiers:

- Basic (from B1 to B2)

- Standard (from S0 to S9v2)

I never use the Basic tier. It is far too limited, even for development. It only allows for small models, with simple refresh, no perspectives, no partitions, and no Direct Query. This is not helpful when you are needing to develop for systems deployed in the Standard tier.

The equivalent of Service Level Objectives (SLOs) for AAS is pricing tiers. Standard offers a range of pricing tiers ranging from S0 to S9v2. A key advantage of AAS is the ability to scale it up and down as required, and to pause and resume it. You can pause it to save money. I often use AAS in development environments and pause it when it is not in use.

The ability to scale both AAS and the associated Azure SQL databases as required, is very powerful. At many sites, particularly those that only load data once or twice a day, I keep the resources at low SLOs (or pricing tiers) most of the time, and scale them up when required, do the work, and scale them back down. Automating that process has saved my customers large amounts of money.

Working with AAS provides a richer experience than working with SSAS. I also expect to see additional changes and offerings to AAS soon.

PBI-P is a premium workspace within the Power BI service. It is appropriate for customers with larger numbers of users. The current break-even price point is around 500 users. Over time PBI-P is becoming a superset of AAS but it is not yet a replacement, at least not for all my customers. It uses the same client libraries and protocols as AAS and offers paginated reports.

If you need operational reports (rather than strategic reports), do not discount the use of SQL Server Reporting Services (SSRS). There are still many scenarios where it is a better choice than paginated reports in the PBI-P service. If you need to learn about SSRS, we have a dedicated online course at our site: https://training.sqldownunder.com.

One concern that I have with PBI-P is that many of the features that are currently being delivered, particularly in relation to data integration, are edited and managed only in the service using a browser, and do not link to any form of source or version control at all. For end users and proof of concept work, that is excellent. For enterprise development, not so much.

Power BI Premium Per User (PBI-PPU) is an interesting additional offering. The challenge with it at present is that it really is designed for users, not for use as a service. When I am working with enterprises, the limitations that this leads to are not workable for me. I hope this will change.

Tabular Projects and Source Control

Analysis Services Project Tooling

The primary tool provided by Microsoft for building tabular data models is Visual Studio (VS). The models that you build with VS can be deployed to SSAS, to AAS, and to PBI-P.

Earlier versions of the tooling for Analysis Services (and for Integration Services and Reporting Services) were called SQL Server Data Tools (SSDT), and to avoid confusion with tools for building databases, often SQL Server Data Tools – BI. (Really early versions were called Business Intelligence Development Studio).

Up to the VS2017 version, SSDT was available as a standalone tool. It could be installed without the need to already have VS installed. If you already had VS, it would just add a series of project templates. If you did not already have VS installed, it would automatically install the VS shell (known as the partner edition) and then add the project templates.

From VS2019 onwards, you already need to have VS installed; then you add the Analysis Services Projects extension to VS. (And the same for the Reporting Services Projects extension and the Integration Services Projects extension if you need to work with those as well). If you do not already have a license for VS2019, you can install the free VS2019 Community Edition. I am not a lawyer, but my current reading of the license agreement is that even though the Community Edition is not normally licensed for enterprise use, you can use it as a shell for adding these BI extensions.

Projects and Source Control

Your tabular data model projects should be stored in source control. Git-based source control systems work well for this, and either Azure DevOps (AzDO) or GitHub would be good choices. Visual Studio has good integration with Git. There is now a top-level menu item for Git:

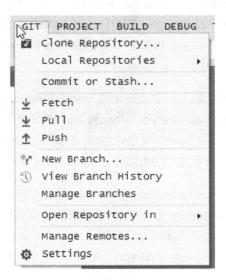

Previously, changes were dealt with using the Team Explorer pane. Now changes are managed using the Git Changes pane:

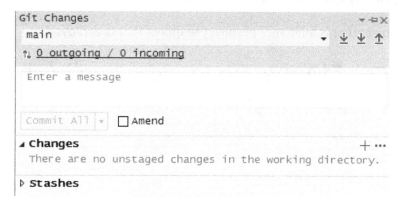

I find that the easiest way to start creating a tabular data model project is to:

- Create a Git repository

- Edit the README file in the repository to reflect what it will be used for

- Clone the repository to your local machine

- Open the local repository in VS

- Use the Add project dialog to then add a new project to the repository

Creating Projects and Solutions

In Visual Studio, projects are created within solutions. The solution is the top-level item, and it can contain multiple projects. Not all the projects in the solution need to be of the same type. For example, I can create a Sales Analytics solution, and within it, I could have a Sales Reporting (SSRS) project, a Sales Analysis (SSAS) project, and more. Make sure though, that you only include projects that are closely related in a single solution.

A project is the object that is built and, usually, the object that is deployed.

Configure your new project

Analysis Services Tabular Project

Project name

```
PopkornKrazeDW Data Model
```

Location

```
C:\Temp
```

Solution name ⓘ

```
PopkornKrazeDW Analytics
```

☐ Place solution and project in the same directory

Framework

```
.NET Framework 4.7.2
```

In the figure above, I am creating a project named PopkornKrazeDW Data Model within the solution named PopkornKrazeDW Analytics. The location for the files would not normally be C:\Temp as shown, but a location within the local copy of the Git repository that I have cloned to start this project creation.

When an Analysis Services Tabular project has been created, you will see that the main file has a .bim extension.

Configuring Workspace Databases

When you are building a tabular data model project, the designer needs access to an Analysis Services database of some type, to hold the data you are working on. Note that this concept is entirely separate to the database (and server) that you will later deploy your data model to. It might be the same, but it often will not be.

There are three locations that can be used for this database:

- Local SQL Server Analysis Services
- Azure Analysis Services
- Integrated Workspace

You might have a local installation of SSAS that you can use, and you might have an AAS server that you can use, but my preference in almost every case, is to use the Integrated Workspace. This workspace is an in-memory implementation of Analysis Services that is launched as a child process to your copy of Visual Studio.

If you have not already configured this, the first time you open an Analysis Services project, you will be asked which workspace database you want to use.

In the Tools menu, under Options, and then Analysis Services Tabular, you can choose the default location for workspace databases:

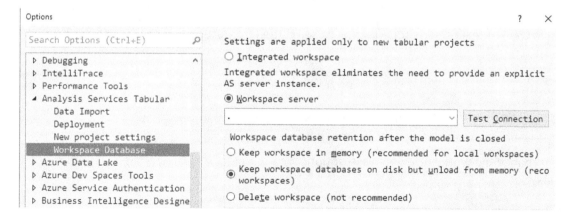

You can also choose whether the workspace data is kept when you close VS, to make it easier to restart again later.

For your current project, you can see which option is being used by right-clicking the .bim file in Solution Explorer and choosing Properties:

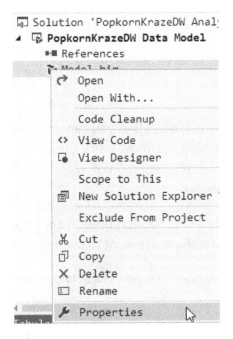

Look in the Properties pane for a setting to see if the Integrated Workspace is being used or not:

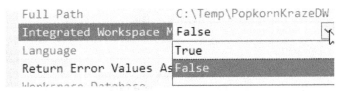

If you change the workspace database options for a .bim file, VS will need to close and reopen the project.

Configuring Compatibility Level

Another important setting that you should check when creating a new project is the Compatibility Level. This determines the level of language support that the model will support. And for SSAS, this will indicate the version of SSAS that you are targeting.

In the Properties for the .bim file, there is a setting for this:

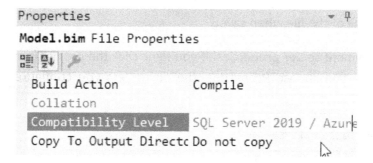

And, like you can for the workspace database, you can set a default value to use for new projects, in the Tools menu, under Analysis Services Tabular, then New project settings:

Configuring Data Model Properties

The final set of properties that I configure on new projects are the data model properties.

First, I like to rename the .bim file in Solution Explorer from Model.bim to something more meaningful:

That will be the name of the file when saved.

I also set the deployment server properties. If you right-click the project (note: not the .bim file) in Solution Explorer and choose Properties, the dialog lets you configure these deployment properties:

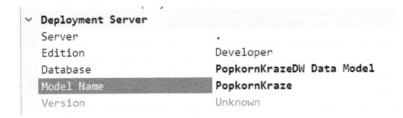

In this dialog, I set the following:

- Server – this is the server that I will later deploy the project to. In this case, I put a single period, and that is shorthand for the local default SSAS server, but generally, this would be the address of an AAS server.

- Database – the database name will default to the name of your project. You might want to change it.

- Model Name – defaults to Model. I prefer to have a more meaningful name as users will see this name when connecting.

Multi-User Development

Note that the Analysis Services Project options in Visual Studio do not lend themselves well to multi-user development.

When you are developing the model, you are modifying the .bim file. From the perspective of the source control system, there is one file that is being changed. Having that changed by multiple developers and in inconsistent ways at the same time is a challenge.

I see three options here:

- Allowing multiple developers to work at the same time and then manually merging the changes into a single branch. This is painful but can often be done. The .bim file is basically a large JSON file that can be merged to some degree, particularly if some developers are only adding measures, etc.

- Only allowing a single developer to work on a single model at one time. For many sites, this works well. Developers can work concurrently but only on different data models.

- Using Tabular Editor to shred the .bim file into a folder of separate JSON files that live in source control; do most of the work within Tabular Editor, and then use it to reassemble a .bim file that is later deployed. (Or deploy just the individual files)

Initial Loading of Tables

Authentication to Analysis Services

If you are using Analysis Services, you need to be able to connect to it. Users might need to connect using tools like Excel, developers might need to connect using tools like SSRS, and other users might need to connect to administer the server.

In SQL Server Management Studio, there are options for connecting to Analysis Services:

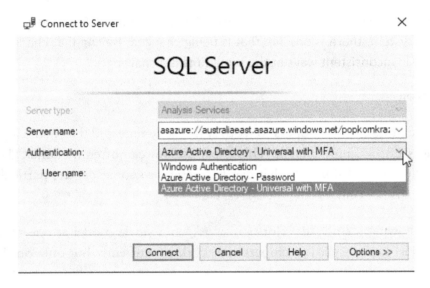

Windows Authentication is what you need if you are connecting to SSAS on-premises.

Azure Active Directory – Universal with MFA is the option that I most often use to connect to AAS.

Authentication to Data Sources

AAS also needs to be authenticated when it connects to data sources such as databases. It allows you to configure separate credentials and connection details for each data source. You might also need to update those details on the AAS server after a deployment, depending upon whether you use different credentials during development.

When an Analysis Services Project needs to connect to a data source, it gives you a small number of options. Most times, I will let it store a username and password for making the connection. For databases, I wish I did not need to do this.

I mentioned earlier in the book that ADF has its own managed service identity and that we could use that to connect to resources. Unfortunately, AAS does not expose a similar identity. I do wish it did provide one. It would avoid needing to deal with usernames and passwords.

Important: The user that I use for connecting from an Analysis Services Project to my data warehouse database, is a user who is only given permission to SELECT and EXECUTE on the Analytics schema.

Selecting and Transforming the Tables

Because the hard work has already been done in creating the Analytics views, once I have authenticated the tabular data model project to the data source (i.e., the data warehouse database), I will see a list of views from the Analytics schema, as they are the only objects that the authenticated user can see.

I just select all these views.

In the navigator, instead of clicking **Load**, I click Transform. This is not because I want to perform any transformations using Power Query at this point, but because I want to rename the tables. Unfortunately, neither the project nor Power BI give you an option (at present) to stop it pre-pending the schema name to the front of the table names. So, a view called Customer in the Analytics schema will be loaded as a table called Analytics Customer. So, I must rename all the tables to remove the Analytics prefix. This is another aspect that I hope will change at some point.

Initial Commit to Git

Once I get to this point in creating a project, I usually make my initial commit to the source code repository.

Before making the commit, ensure that VS has added an appropriate **.gitignore** file to your solution so that you are not always seeing changes to files that really do not matter.

Core Aspects of Tabular Models

In this section, I will describe the basic changes that I make to the tabular data model projects. The more of this that you do a great job on, the more your users will like your data model.

Relationships

Now that the tables are loaded, I create relationships.

In these data models, relationships must be based on single columns. When I am designing the underlying DataModel tables, I have already ensured that my relationships have been created that way.

You can work in the Relationships view of the designer, and drag columns to form relationships, or use the Edit Relationship right-click option to create the required relationships:

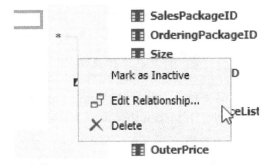

You can open the Manage Relationships dialog and manage them all at once:

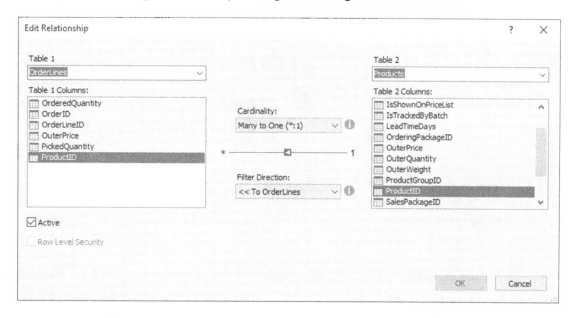

Whichever way you create the relationships, make sure that the cardinality is correct. A very common mistake that I see, is that users create relationships when the tables are empty, and the designer defaults the relationship as one-to-one. That is rarely correct.

Relationships can also be defined as Active or Inactive. I do not like the name that the team chose for this. An Active relationship is more like a default relationship. If an Order table has an Order Date and a Delivery Date, if the relationship from Order Date to the Date table is active, then, by default, when you analyze orders by date, the system will use the Order Date. But you can choose to still analyze orders by Delivery Date if you want to, using Inactive relationship.

In the designer, Inactive relationships are shown with dotted lines:

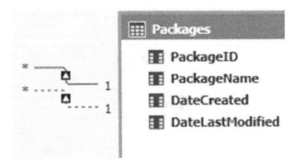

Calculated Tables

If I am going to be regularly working with multiple relationships to the same table, I might decide to create some calculated tables.

For example, in the example that I mentioned before, where an Order has an Order Date and a Delivery Date, I might choose to create a Delivery Date table and, instead of making the inactive relationship to the Date table, I would make the relationship to the Delivery Date table.

Note: I would not do that for every date in a table that has many dates. It only makes sense to do this for dates that are regularly used for filtering, and that might be filtered concurrently with other dates.

If I have a table called Date (as I usually do), I could create a calculated Delivery Date table by using the expression:

=ALLNOBLANKROWS(Date)

Hiding Columns and Tables from Clients

Not all columns should be visible to client applications. It is important to constantly strive to simplify the data model that you present to users. Hiding columns and tables can help with this.

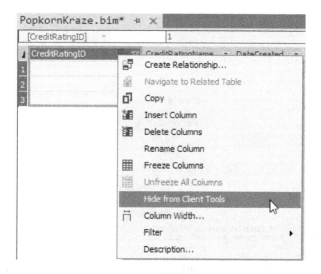

I usually hide all the key columns. In my Analytics views, they are columns that end with the suffix Key.

I will also hide columns that should only be exposed using measures.

Make sure that you do not just hide columns that you do not need in the data model. If you really do not need the columns, delete the columns instead. You need to keep your data models as small and optimized as possible.

Apart from columns, you can also hide entire tables.

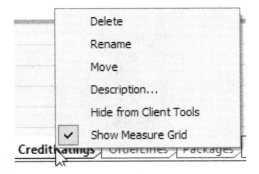

I often hide tables that are only used for linking other tables, or where I needed to denormalize data for some reason.

Measures

In every data model, I create a set of standard measures. A good example is that most tables will benefit from having a measure that provides a count of the rows in the table.

Measures can be explicit or implicit.

Explicit measures are created using DAX.

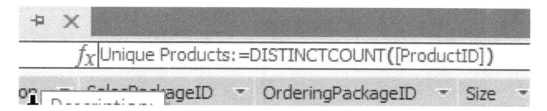

Figure 10-17 Explicit Measure

The designer provides a set of auto-sum options to help you to create basic measures:

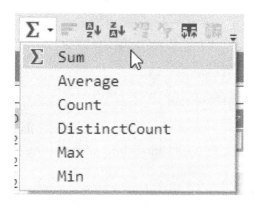

Summarization for Columns

The other type of measure is an implicit measure. These are created by the client tool. For example, if I drag a numeric column onto a report, and a measure is needed, by default, the client tool will give me the SUM of the column.

That might be entirely wrong. For example, if the column indicates the size of a product, adding up the size might make no sense at all.

You can create the default aggregate that the tools use by configuring the summarization for a column.

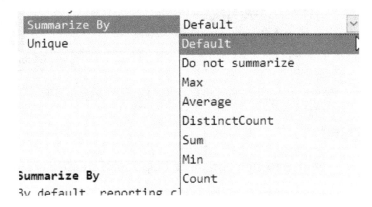

For this example, a DistinctCount might work better. For many columns, configuring Do not summarize might be the best option.

Correct Level for Computations

I have had many clients ask me, that if they can create a calculated column in the DataModel tables, or in the Analytics views, in the tabular data model using DAX, or in a client tool, where should they be created?

Try to always create computations at the lowest level of the stack where they might be reused. This can be very important for drill-downs. If the user sees a value at one level, and drills down but can no longer see the value, this can be very confusing for them.

Mark as Date Table

It is rare for me to create a tabular data model that does not have a Date table. I have seen them but almost every model needs to have a way of knowing when actions or events occurred.

In the examples I have used so far in the book, you will notice that I will have a table called Date already loaded. But it is important to understand that even though I think of it as a date table, the tabular data model does not know that it is one. It just happens to be a table with the name Date.

Before time intelligence functions will work as expected, you need to tell the tabular data model which table is the date table, and which column holds the date.

If you have the Date table selected, from the menu, you can choose an option to set it as the date table:

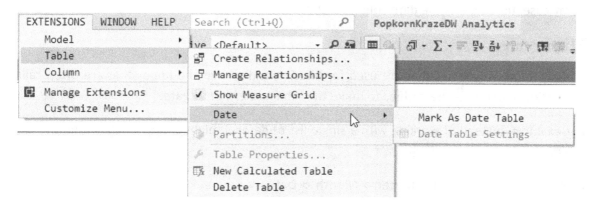

Once you choose to set the table as the date table, you will be asked which column holds a date:

In my case, the name of the date column is Date.

Hierarchies

It is common with tables that are used for filtering and slicing (the tables that are often called dimensions), to create hierarchies to make the table easier to navigate.

For example, instead of working with a single list of dates, I might create levels within the Date table:

Calendar Year -> Calendar Quarter -> Month -> Date

And I might create other hierarchies on the same table:

Fiscal Year -> Fiscal Quarter -> Month -> Date

Columns might appear in more than one hierarchy.

Data Formats

Each column has a default format. For some columns, you need to ensure that an appropriate format is being used.

For example, DAX has a datetime data type. It does not have a date data type nor a time data type. The default format for a datetime data type is to just display the date.

If you are expecting a time to appear, you will need to change the format:

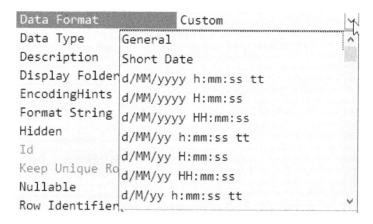

Data Categories

As well as data types, columns can have data categories. Configuring these correctly can make a big difference to users of your data model.

Power BI and other tools can make really good use of data that they know is of a certain category. You can configure data categories in the column properties:

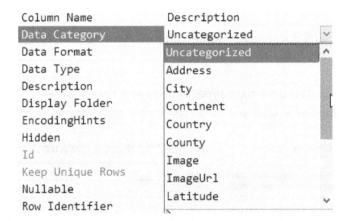

Report Measure Table

Measures can be placed in many locations within reports. To try to provide some structure, I often create a static table called Report Measure by using DAX, within the data model:

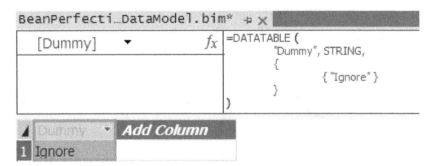

I have a single column called Dummy and that column is hidden. The table is not hidden but the only column is hidden. This will be an anchor point for adding measures in end-user reports.

Testing and Deployment Options

Testing During Development

While you are developing a tabular data model, you will often want to see how the model will appear to a user.

You could connect from SQL Server Management Studio (SSMS) to a deployed project but unfortunately the data model browser in SSMS is now quite poor. One key limitation is that it does not include column groups.

A better option is to use Excel to connect to the data model for testing:

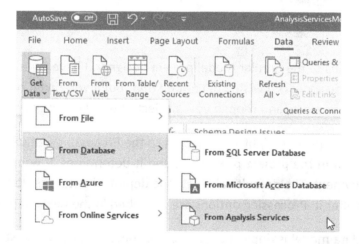

Excel has an option to connect to Analysis Services, and that will work fine. An easier option though, is that both the tabular model editor in VS and SSMS both include a small icon that lets you see the model using Excel. When you do that, it automatically takes care of connecting you to the correct model.

Deployment

To deploy a tabular data model, you can right-click the project in Solution Explorer and choose Deploy:

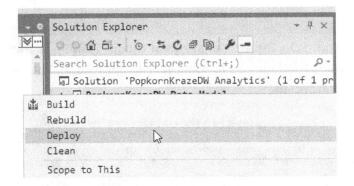

In some recent versions of the tabular model project designer, I have seen situations where that Deploy menu option disappears. I wish it did not do that, but if you find it has disappeared, there is no option but to save, close, and reopen your project. It usually reappears at that point.

Before you deploy though, you might want to choose the Processing Option for the deployment. This is another option in the project properties, and it determines how much data loading will happen after deployment. The default value lets the deployed database decide that for you, but you might want to alter it. Processing options are described in the next chapter.

Once the tabular data model is deployed, you can connect to it using the standard tools: Excel, SSMS, and Power BI.

Chapter 11: Using Advanced Tabular Model Techniques

Overview

In this chapter, I will discuss a few more advanced, yet important concepts for working with tabular data models.

I will start by describing how processing works, and the different types of processing, then delve into security. I will describe how I apply row level security, and if necessary, object level security. Labeling sensitive data is fast becoming important for many organizations. It can be applied in the Power BI service but not in tabular data models at this time.

Awesome image by John Salvino

Finally, I will look at areas that can improve your tabular data model designs. That includes perspective, translations, partitioning for performance, optimizing data model size, working around parent-child and many to many relationships, and checking for best practices.

Processing Data Models

Processing is the way that data gets loaded into tabular data models. There are others, but the main tasks that happen during processing are:

- Loading data into tables

- Creating hierarchies

- Recalculating calculated objects

- Recreating relationships

Keep in mind that processing can fail. Common causes of processing failure are:

- Underlying system, database, or network issues

- Authentication failures to data sources

- Insufficient memory

- Data issues (for example, a column that is marked as unique has loaded non-unique data)

Not all processing options are available in each service.

Database Processing Option – Default

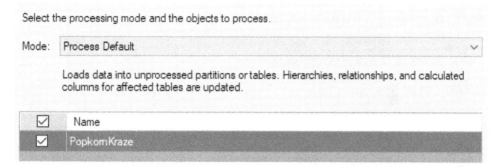

This processing option detects the current process state for each object, then performs the minimum work required to bring all objects to a processed state.

If a table is empty, it is loaded.

Later, hierarchies, calculated objects, and relationships are rebuilt.

Database Processing Option – Full

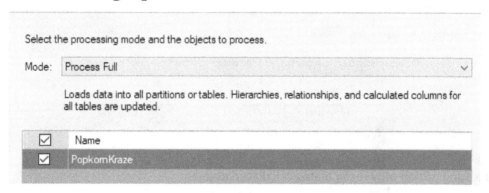

This processing option starts by clearing and reloading data for all objects. It then rebuilds hierarchies, calculated objects, and relationships.

This option uses the most resources and is required whenever you have made structural changes to a deployed data model.

Database Processing Option – Clear

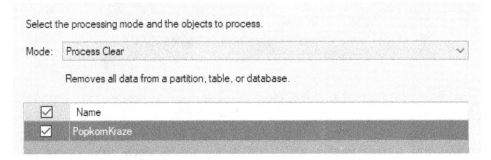

This processing option clears data from all objects.

The definition of the objects (i.e., the metadata) is left unchanged.

Database Processing Option – Recalc

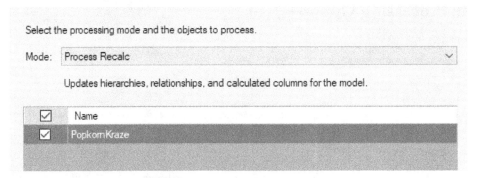

This processing option only recalculates calculated objects.

No data loading is performed.

Table Processing Options

Tables have some similar processing options, but there are also additional processing options:

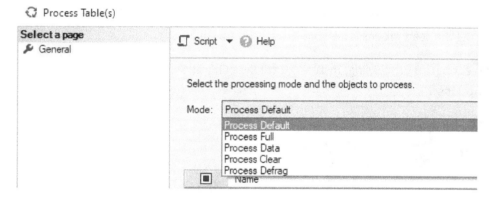

The Process Data option clears and loads all table data.

The Process Defrag option is a special option used to defragment auxiliary table indexes.

Instead of processing an entire table, it is also possible to process a single partition of a table. Partitioning will be discussed later in this chapter.

Scripting Processing Steps

While you can use tools like SSMS to process tabular data model objects, you can also use it to create scripts that can process the objects programmatically.

When you configure processing, instead of clicking OK, at the top of the window, note there are scripting options:

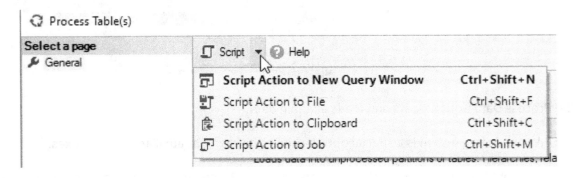

An example processing script is shown here:

```
{
  "refresh": {
    "type": "full",
    "objects": [
      {
        "database": "PopkornKrazeDataModel",
        "table": "Product"
      }
    ]
  }
}
```

The command for processing is "refresh". The type selected here is the processing type of "full". The object is the Product table in the PopkornKrazeDataModel database.

The list of objects is an array and can contain many objects.

Scheduling Processing

The mechanism that I use for scheduling processing depends upon where the tabular data model is deployed.

On-Premises or VM-Based – SQL Server Agent

The main scheduling tool for SQL Server systems is SQL Server Agent. It can be used to schedule processing of tabular data models.

In Object Explorer in SSMS, you can connect to SQL Server Agent and see a list of jobs that have been configured:

```
⊟ 🖥 SQL Server Agent
  ⊟ 📁 Jobs
       ⊞ Agent history clean up: distribut
       ⊞ Distribution clean up: distributi
       ⊞ Do Something Daily
       ⊞ Monitor and sync replication ager
       ⊞ Reinitialize subscriptions having
       ⊞ Replication agents checkup
       ⊞ Replication monitoring refresher
       ⊞ SSIS Server Maintenance Job
       ⊞ syspolicy_purge_history
     ⚙ Job Activity Monitor
```

When you create a new job, you can add different types of job steps:

```
Type:
┌─────────────────────────────────────────────────┐
│ Transact-SQL script (T-SQL)                     │
├─────────────────────────────────────────────────┤
│ Operating system (CmdExec)                      │
│ PowerShell                                      │
│ Replication Distributor                         │
│ Replication Merge                               │
│ Replication Queue Reader                        │
│ Replication Snapshot                            │
│ Replication Transaction-Log Reader              │
│ SQL Server Analysis Services Command            │
│ SQL Server Analysis Services Query              │
│ SQL Server Integration Services Package         │
│ Transact-SQL script (T-SQL)                     │
└─────────────────────────────────────────────────┘
```

You can add the scripts that I showed you how to generate earlier, as SQL Server Analysis Services Command job steps.

SQL Server Agent jobs can also be executed by enterprise schedulers rather than by the built-in scheduler.

On-Premises or VM-Based – Integration Services

If you are using SSIS, it is even easier to set up processing. SSIS includes a built-in Analysis Services Processing Task:

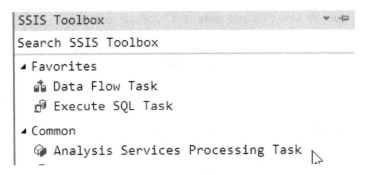

SSIS also includes another Analysis Services task that can be used to execute DDL (data definition language) tasks:

This task can make it easier to perform operations that change the structure of the database like rearranging table partitions.

SSIS packages can then be scheduled either by SQL Server Agent or an enterprise scheduler.

Azure Data Factory Based Processing

At the time of writing, ADF does not include a dedicated task for processing tabular data models in Analysis Services. Given how highly voted the request to add this is, I expect to see this added soon.

While you could create an SSIS package to do the processing and load it into ADF, I prefer to use native ADF capabilities to control the processing.

AAS has a REST API that can be used to control the processing. It is documented here:

https://docs.microsoft.com/en-us/rest/api/datafactory/v2

An example ADF pipeline that can be used to perform the processing looks like this:

You can find the code for the pipeline and details of how to use it at this link:

https://github.com/furmangg/automating-azure-analysis-services/blob/master/README.md#processazureas

Before you can use ADF to perform the processing, you will need to add ADF's managed service identity as an administrator for AAS, as described earlier in the book. For tighter security, you could add it to a role that has Process permission instead.

Implementing Row Level Security

As with all things in Windows and Azure, you should add groups to roles, not users. Let someone else in the organization make decisions about how is in which group. Try to stay out of assigning permissions to individual users. The structure should always be:

- Roles are created

- Permissions are assigned to Roles

- Groups are added to Roles

- Users are added to Groups (by someone else, not in the project)

Managing Roles

While you could configure roles in the deployed tabular data model, the best place to configure them is within your tabular data model project while you are designing it. A common mistake that I see is when role membership is changed on the deployed data model, and when a new deployment occurs, those role assignments are overwritten by what was configured in the project.

The Model menu has an option for managing roles:

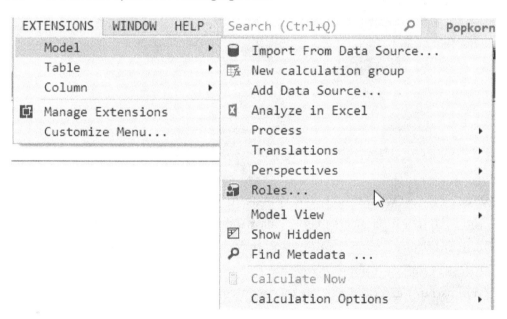

Role Database Permissions

When you create a role, you can assign it the following permissions to the entire database:

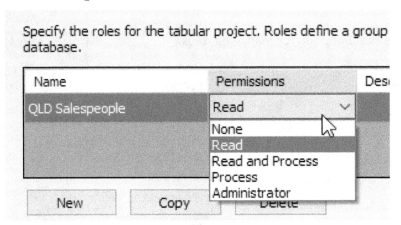

- None does just what it says. The role has no permission.
- Read is all that most users need. It allows them to browse the data.
- Read and Process allows reading and processing.
- Process is for controlling processing.
- Administrator can do whatever they want.

Role Members

Once the role is created, you can add members to the role:

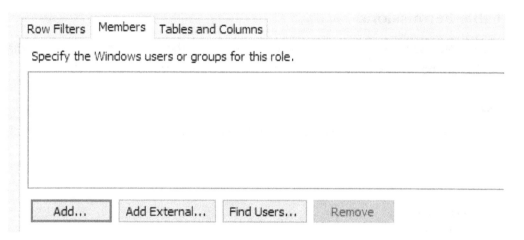

This window was originally designed for on-premises work with an organizational domain. You can still use it to add domain groups (or users if you must) and that will work if you have a hybrid Active Directory set up.

Generally, I am looking to add Azure AD groups, and these will not appear if you just click Add. Instead, click Add External and enter the email address of the group (or user).

Role Table Permissions

A role's overall access to the data model is determined by the database permissions that were assigned. This can be further limited by configuring the Tables and Columns list:

Row Filters	Members	Tables and Columns

Select Tables and Columns that should not be visible to users. Calculation groups are currently not supported.

- ⊞ ☐ Cinemas
- ⊞ ☐ Orders
- ⊞ ☐ Products
- ⊞ ☐ CinemaGroups
- ⊞ ☐ CreditRatings

I do not particularly like this dialog. Many developers miss the fact that it is apply negative logic i.e., it is asking you which tables and columns should **not** be visible to the users of the role. It is easy to assume it is asking you which tables and columns you want them to see.

Role Row Filters

You can also limit which rows of a table that members of a role can see:

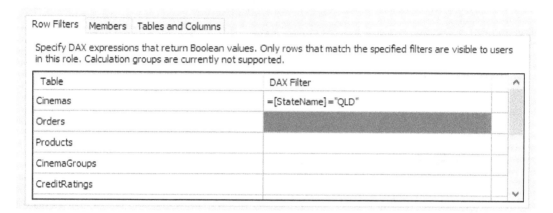

In this dialog, the role members can see all rows in any table that does not have a DAX Filter specified. Where there is an expression, that expression limits the rows from that table that the role member can see. In the example above, the Cinemas table is being restricted to only those in the state of QLD.

Try to avoid using overly complex DAX expressions for row filters.

Dynamic User Security

It is possible to create DAX expressions that refer to the user who is connected and make security decisions based upon those identities. These filters typically use the DAX USERNAME function.

Try to avoid ever doing this.

You do not want to have your model containing a series of expressions that refer to specific users.

There are scenarios where I have created dynamic security, but it is usually related to using Power BI Embedded and works by using the CUSTOMDATA function. This might be necessary if you have users authenticated by Azure Active Directory B2C (Business to Consumer).

Testing Roles and Row Filters

Once you have configured roles and filters, you can test them by using several options.

In Visual Studio, if you use the Analyze in Excel option, the dialog allows you to configure roles to use for browsing:

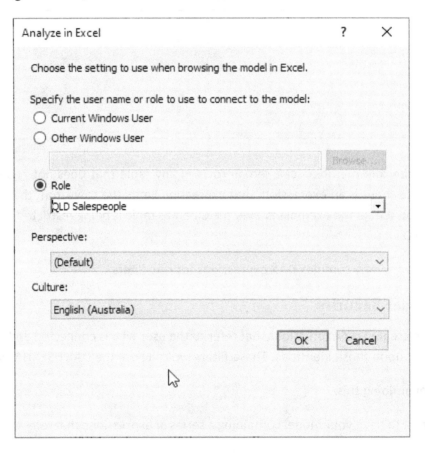

This same window will allow you to choose multiple roles at the same time. This is useful because users can be members of multiple roles via their group memberships.

If you are using the Browse option in SQL Server Management Studio, you can also set the security context, and in particular, the roles. There is a small icon showing a person in the top-left of the dialog:

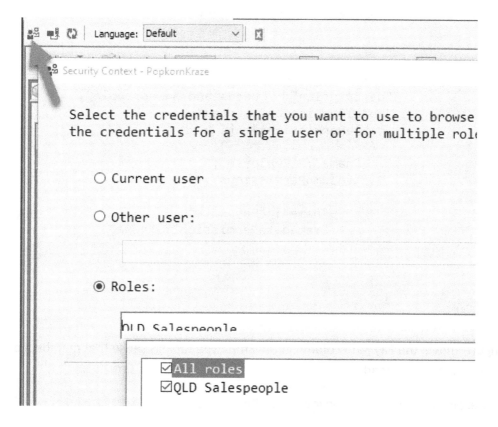

Object Level Security

Tabular data models also can configure security at the object level. This allows hiding of sensitive tables and columns. At the time of writing, no graphical interface has been provided for making these configurations. They need to be configured directly in the JSON contained in the .bim file.

```
"roles": [
  {
    "name": "QLD Salespeople",
    "description": "Queensland Salespeople",
    "modelPermission": "read",
    "tablePermissions": [
      {
        "name": "Employee",
        "columnPermissions": [
          {
            "name": "Pay Rate",
            "metadataPermission": "none"
          }
        ]
      }
    ]
  }
}
```

In the figure above, the Pay Rate column in the Employee table is set so that members of the QLD Salespeople role cannot read it.

Note: Object level security and role level security cannot be combined.

Labeling Sensitive Data

Power BI has recently added the ability to apply labels to sensitive data. When the setting is enabled, Microsoft Information Protection sensitivity labels that have been configured at the organization level can be applied within Power BI. This option is not available within the tabular data model designer.

Perspectives

You will need to find a balance between having a single complex data model, and a series of smaller data models.

One way of reducing complexity for your users is to configure Perspectives:

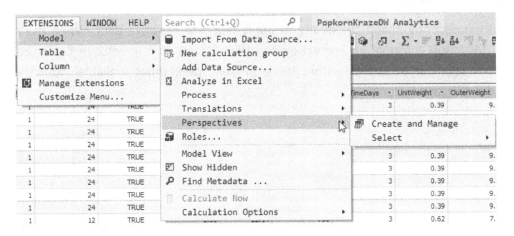

A perspective is a simplified way of viewing the same data model. You give the perspective a name, and then choose which data items will appear to someone connected to the perspective:

Perspectives

Use perspectives to define views of the data. Perspectives make it easier to navigate large data sets.

New Perspective

Fields	SalesData
- **Tables**	▣
- CinemaGroups	▣
CinemaGroupID	☐
CinemaGroupName	☑
CinemaGroupShortCode	☐
DateCreated	☐
DateLastModified	☐
+ Cinemas	☐
+ CreditRatings	☐
+ OrderLines	☐
+ Orders	☑

Instead of connecting to the data model from their client tools, the users connect to the perspective. It will appear as another data model name in the same database.

This can be useful when you want to avoid overloading a user with too much information. It is important to note though, that while it might look like it would stop a user from getting to data that is not part of the perspective, that is not the case. A user can still access other tables by using DAX formulas. Perspectives are not a security feature.

Translations

You might also need to work with users who want to interact with the tabular data model in different languages. Translations allow you to do this.

Each data model has a default language. It will return the objects with the same names that you define.

You can also choose to manage other language translations:

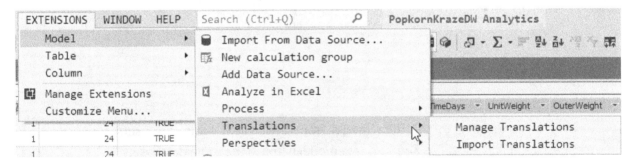

In this system, you will be presented with a list of languages that you can manage:

Manage translations

Specifies the languages for which you are providing translated string:
current string translations already in the model if they exist.

Available Languages:

```
Afar (Djibouti) -- (aa-DJ)
Afar (Eritrea) -- (aa-ER)
Afar (Ethiopia) -- (aa-ET)
Afrikaans (Namibia) -- (af-NA)
Afrikaans (South Africa) -- (af-ZA)
Aghem (Cameroon) -- (agq-CM)
Akan (Ghana) -- (ak-GH)
Albanian (Albania) -- (sq-AL)
Albanian (Kosovo) -- (sq-XK)
Albanian (North Macedonia) -- (sq-MK)
Alsatian (France) -- (gsw-FR)
Alsatian (Liechtenstein) -- (gsw-LI)
Alsatian (Switzerland) -- (gsw-CH)
Amharic (Ethiopia) -- (am-ET)
Arabic (Algeria) -- (ar-DZ)
Arabic (Bahrain) -- (ar-BH)
Arabic (Chad) -- (ar-TD)
Arabic (Comoros) -- (ar-KM)
Arabic (Djibouti) -- (ar-DJ)
```

You can pick a set of languages to work with, and then export the language file. The exported file will contain a large amount of JSON. For each element that has a name in your data model, it will include an element that shows the default label.

For each additional language that you selected, it will have another set of the same elements to provide you an option to change the labels.

You do not need to change all the labels. Any label that you do not provide a translation for, will use the default label.

Once you have edited the file to suit your requirements, you can then import the language file and your language changes will then take effect when you deploy the model.

The data model browsers in VS and SSMS both provide options for you to choose another language to use when viewing the data model.

Scripting Database with TMSL

If you have worked with SQL Server or any relational database in the past, you will know that you can generate a script to create the database and all the objects that it contains.

The equivalent for databases holding tabular data models is to create a TMSL (Tabular Model Scripting Language) script:

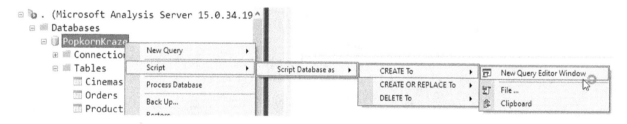

The following figure shows an example of part of the TMSL script:

```json
{
  "create": {
    "database": {
      "name": "PopkornKraze",
      "compatibilityLevel": 1500,
      "model": {
        "name": "PopkornKraze",
        "culture": "en-AU",
        "dataSources": [
          {
            "type": "structured",
            "name": "SQL/ ;PopkornKraze",
            "connectionDetails": {
              "protocol": "tds",
              "address": {
                "server": ".",
                "database": "PopkornKraze"
              },
              "authentication": null,
              "query": null
            },
            "credential": {
              "AuthenticationKind": "ServiceAccount",
              "EncryptConnection": false
            }
          }
        ],
        "tables": [
          {
            "name": "Cinemas",
            "columns": [
              {
                "name": "CinemaID",
                "dataType": "int64",
                "sourceColumn": "CinemaID"
              },
```

Partitioning Data

When data volumes grow large, it can be time to consider using partitions. There are two levels at which partitions can be applied:

- Database tables

- Tabular data model

Both can be effective.

Database Table Partitions

This concept only applies to database data sources. SQL Server supports a concept of range partitions. (Some other databases support different mechanisms like hash partitions). A range partition scheme has left or right boundaries and determines the data that lives in each partition.

The most common partitioning scheme in databases uses dates. If a company needs to keep 7 years of data on a rolling basis, they might create a partition for each month in that 7-year period. The advantages of this are:

- A month's worth of data can rapidly be removed from the table (often this only involves milliseconds)

- A month's worth of data could rapidly be added to the table

- A single partition of the table could be truncated if needed.

- Each table partition can have a different compression style. For example, old static data could be page compressed and recent data could be row compressed.

- Table partitions can be made read-only.

There are other advantages as well. While providing many benefits, partitioning table data requires careful design, particularly in relation to indexes.

For more information on table partitioning, refer to the following whitepaper that I was a technical reviewer for:

https://docs.microsoft.com/en-us/previous-versions/sql/sql-server-2008/dd578580(v=sql.100)

It is a detailed reference (over 60 pages) and even though it was prepared for SQL Server 2008, it is still a very relevant reference.

Tabular Data Model Partitions

Many organizations start loading their tabular data models overnight but as the data volume grows, they get to a point where it takes too long to load all the data. Tables in tabular data models can also have partitions and this can be used to improve the situation.

Not all editions of Analysis Services support partitions. To make reasonable use of partitions, you need to be using either the Enterprise Edition of SQL Server Analysis Services or at least the Standard Tier of Azure Analysis Services.

Every table in a tabular data model contains at least one partition. By default, that is the entire table. But you can manage the partitions for a table:

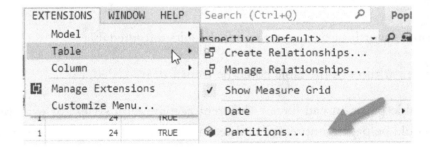

When you first open this dialog for a table, it will show a single partition named Partition:

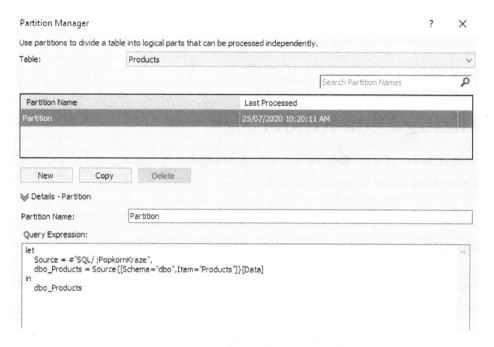

In this dialog, you can configure additional partitions for a table. Mostly, partitions will cover different time periods.

Each partition can have a separate query source, but the queries must be compatible i.e., they must return the same columns, so that the union of all the tables can be combined to create a single table.

Table Partition Example

As a simple example, I worked on a system where the entire table was loaded every Sunday, and every other day, the "This Week" partition was loaded.

As another example, I worked on a system where the entire table was loaded at 2AM each day, and all day long, every half hour, the "Today" partition was loaded.

I do not like systems where the tabular data model is loaded every half hour, but some customers require this.

Optimizing Data Model Size

To keep performance of your tabular data models high, it is important to constantly work to minimize the overall size of your data models.

Minimizing Data Model Size

The basic rules that I apply for keeping data model sizes in check are:

- Do not load tables that are not currently required. (Do not add tables that might be needed later. They can be added later).

- Do not load rows that are not required. (Do not load 7 years of detailed history when detail is only needed for recent months and an aggregate will be suitable for older data).

- Do not load columns that are not required. (Do not just hide unnecessary columns; delete them).

- Think long and hard about the difference between operational reporting vs strategic reporting. (Most operational reporting should not be sourced from a tabular data model).

Using DAX Studio and Vertipaq Analyzer

Vertipaq Analyzer is a popular 3rd party tool that can analyze the structure and performance of tabular data models.

DAX Studio is another popular 3rd party tool that many developers use when writing DAX code. It contains an implementation of Vertipaq Analyzer and makes it easy to use. (The original Vertipaq Analyzer runs from within Excel).

No matter which version you use, make sure that you import the metrics of your data models and see what is consuming the size.

I regularly see data models where two or three columns are responsible for most of the size of a large table. Two very common scenarios tend to bloat the size of data models:

- Storing datetime values with date and time in a single column

- Storing key values for large fact-style tables (or any high cardinality columns)

Those two scenarios alone often account for 70 percent or more of the size of a table.

Configuring Encoding Hints

The tabular data model engine automatically chooses how to encode data values. There are two basic methods:

- Value encoding

- Hash encoding

Text data is always hash encoded.

Numeric data can use either value or hash encoding. Columns that are used in aggregations should be value encoded. Columns that are used for grouping should be hash encoded.

If you notice that the engine is not using the scheme that you think it should be, you can configure encoding hints as part of the properties of a column:

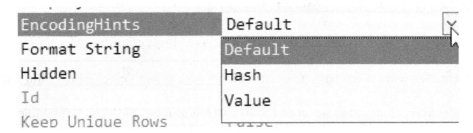

By adjusting the encoding hints that are used, you might be able to improve data model size and performance.

Additional Concepts

As I finish this discussion on tabular data models, there are a further two concepts that I want to mention.

Parent-Child Relationships

In older multi-dimensional models in SQL Server Analysis Services, there was direct support for creating parent-child relationships.

For example, I might have had an employee table, and an employee's manager was also an employee. This means that the table included a natural form of hierarchy, without the need to create a separate hierarchy. While this type of model allowed you to have these relationships, the performance of them was very poor. To avoid this performance hit, I often used a parent-child naturalizer tool to reduce the parent-child relationship back to a standard hierarchy. It was not then as flexible, but it provided a major performance boost.

Tabular data models do not have native support for parent-child relationships. Instead of trying to model these, create a natural hierarchy instead. I realize that it will not be a perfect outcome, but it will let you have a much faster outcome.

Many to Many Relationships

Some data models require many to many relationships. While tools might let you configure these, in my experience, users do not understand the outcomes and using this type of relationship will be problematic.

I encourage you, wherever possible, to try to design many to many relationships out of your models.

Checking for Best Practices

The community and the Power BI team are constantly developing best practices for tabular models as we all gain more and more experience building them.

The following blob post from Michael Kovalsky in the product team is a great summary of some of these best practice rules:

https://powerbi.microsoft.com/en-us/blog/best-practice-rules-to-improve-your-models-performance

Tabular Editor also includes the ability to configure rules for checking best practices. I encourage you to also consider using that to automate these checks.

Chapter 12: Connecting Power BI and Creating Reports

Overview

In all the previous chapters of this book, I have described the framework that I use for implementing Power BI projects in the enterprise.

The core aim is to provide an underlying data model that makes it easy for enterprise users to then create the reports that they need.

In this final chapter, I will describe how the users connect to the data model, and how I suggest that they add measures at the report level.

Finally, I will describe improvements that have been delivered with composite data models.

Awesome image by Yiorgos Ntrahas

Connecting to the Data Model

In Power BI Desktop, when I begin to create a report, if my tabular data model is in Power BI Premium, then I just need to use the Get Data option and select Power BI Datasets. If, however, my data is in Azure Analysis Services (AAS) or in SQL Server Analysis Services (SSAS), then I need to connect to the server.

If my data is in SSAS, in the Get Data menu, I can choose the Analysis Services option:

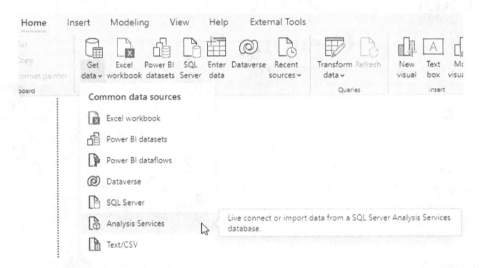

If you are working with SSAS, once your reports are deployed, you will need to have the Enterprise Gateway configured, to allow the Power BI service to connect to the SSAS server within your network.

In this example, I will connect to AAS. That option exists under the Azure section if you select More on the first menu dropdown:

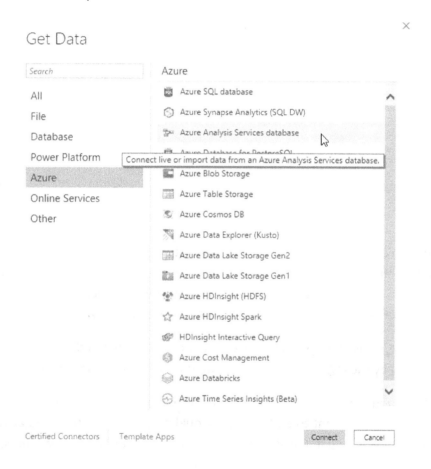

The curious part is that this option leads to the same window as if you had selected the option for SSAS:

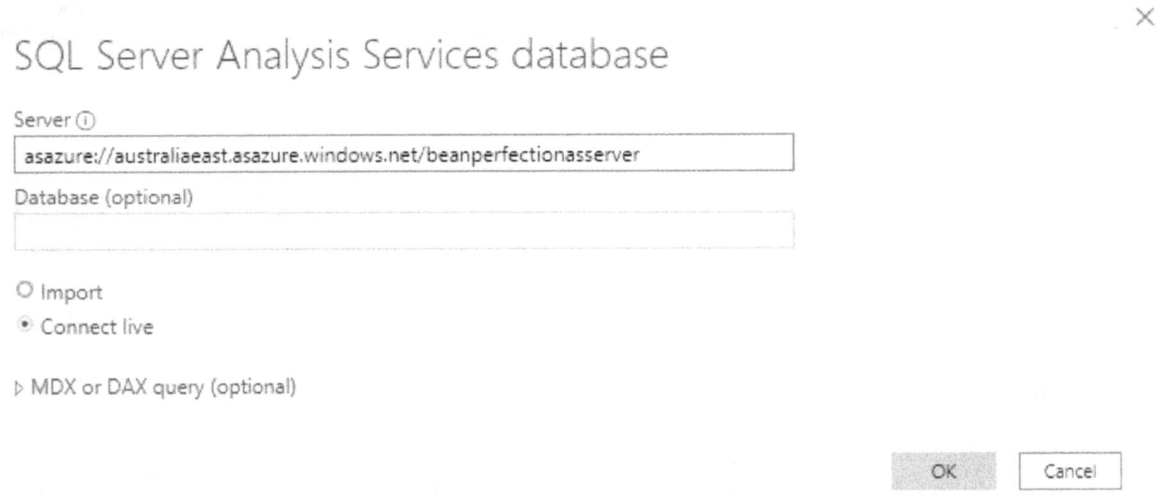

SQL Server Analysis Services database   ✕

Server ⓘ

asazure://australiaeast.asazure.windows.net/beanperfectionasserver

Database (optional)

○ Import
● Connect live

▷ MDX or DAX query (optional)

OK   Cancel

As the AAS service diverges from SSAS, I would suggest that you choose the appropriate option in the menu in case these dialogs also diverge over time. Even though you can use the SQL Server database option to connect to Azure SQL Database, you now get a richer experience if you choose the Azure SQL Database option. I can see the same happening with AAS and SSAS over time.

In the figure above, I have configured the server's address. Notice that the address has an as azure: moniker, followed by the region, then .asazure.windows.net/, and then the server's name.

The dialog allows you to choose Import or Connect live. Import is used if you want to bring all the data into Power BI. If you want to do that, you should be connecting to the Analytics views, and not to the tabular data model. For the models that I have been describing, you should use the Connect live option.

There is an option to use a specific MDX or DAX query at this point. I do not use this option. I consider this the wrong place to be adding and managing queries.

I am then prompted to authenticate:

The authentication dialog will default to Windows but that would only be useful for SSAS. In my case with AAS, I will use the option that says, "Microsoft account". I wish this dialog did not say "Microsoft account" because Microsoft accounts (MSAs) are personal accounts. What this dialog is looking for is what is called an Organizational account (OrgID) which is an Azure Active Directory identity. These are entirely different concepts.

Once I log on to Azure, I can connect. The Navigator is then displayed:

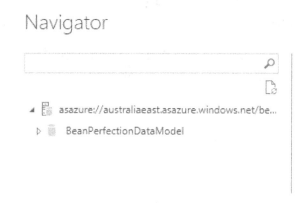

When I expand the BeanPerfectionDataModel database, I can then see the models that I can connect to:

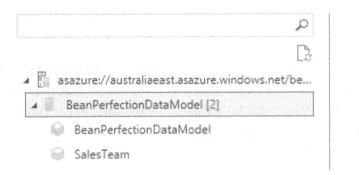

Notice that even though I have a single database, there are two data models shown. The first is the BeanPerfectionDataModel. This is the full data model. You might recall that I renamed it from "Model". I rename the model in the project properties to make it clear which model this is.

The second model SalesTeam is a perspective that I created in the BeanPerfectionDataModel. You can see that it appears like a separate data model within the database.

Once I have connected, the field list from the tabular data model appears and is ready to work with:

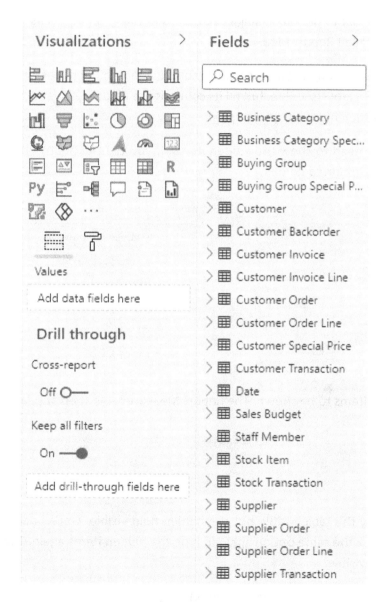

Adding Report Measures

I mentioned earlier that to provide a single location that many report measures can be attached to, I create a table called Report Measure.

The table was not hidden but it contains a single column that is hidden. Because of what I consider a bug in Power BI, if a table is visible, but all its columns are hidden, Power BI also hides the table. That is painful as it then hides my anchor point.

To make it visible, I need to show the hidden items. If you right-click anywhere in the Power BI field list, there is an option to do this:

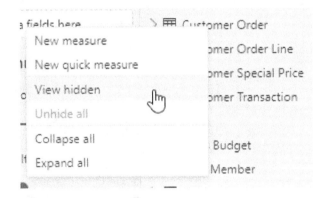

This causes hidden items to be shown. The Report Measure table then appears:

This makes not only the table visible but the hidden field visible. Once I add a measure to this table, I can then click the same option again to hide the hidden items again. The Report Measure table will then stay visible.

I hope this bug in the user interface gets fixed one day.

Using Composite Data Models

I mentioned in an earlier chapter that it is important to set formats for columns, as that is the format that will appear in the data model. What I had not mentioned at that point is that when you are using a Live Connection to Analysis Services, that you could not change the formats locally within reports.

This always seemed a very odd limitation to me. It was explained to me that when you were using the remote data model, there was no local data model within the report, where you could store formats or other changes to the remote model.

Fortunately, that limitation is now being removed. At the time of writing, composite models are in preview and enable you to use a remote model, and a local model at the same time. The local model can be used to modify the remote model.

This will eventually be a standard feature, but I currently need to enable it in Power BI Desktop. From the File menu, select Options and Settings, then Options, and investigate the Preview features:

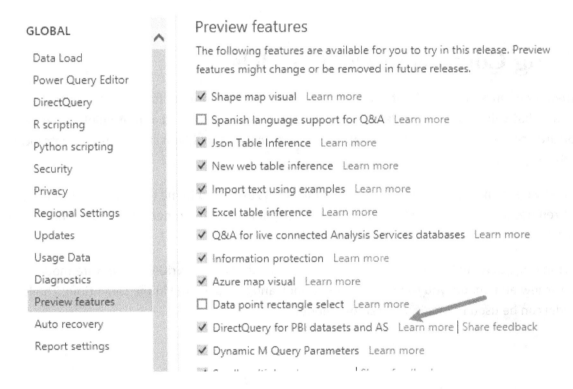

The feature is officially called **DirectQuery for Power BI Datasets and Analysis Services**. You can imagine why we all still call it Composite Models.

Once this feature is enabled, a new option appears on the Modeling tab:

You are then warned about the permanent changes that will then be made:

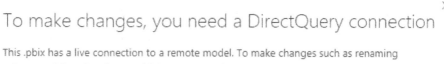

The Live Connection to the remote model will be changed to DirectQuery, but it will then enable you to do the following:

- Rename columns
- Change formats and other properties of columns
- Adding additional data sources

You will notice once the change has been made that when you click on a column, the options at the top of the screen for formatting, etc. are then enabled. With a Live Connection model, they are normally disabled.

On the Relationships tab, all the tables from that same data source will have the same color. You can then add data from additional data sources, and they will be shown in different colors.

Summary

Thanks for reaching the end of this book. I hope you will find the framework that I have described, useful in your own projects, or at least a source of ideas that you might evolve in your own way.

Building great Power BI reports depends upon doing all the underlying work to support those reports. That is where this framework lies.

I mentioned at the start that there is no one right or wrong way to implement Power BI in an enterprise. I have shown you how I do it, and that has been very successful in many projects. Keep in mind though, that Power BI changes rapidly.

I would love to hear from you about your successes and challenges.

Glossary

AAD	Azure Active Directory
AAS	Azure Analysis Services
AD	Active Directory
ADF	Azure Data Factory
ADFS	Active Directory Federation Services
ADS	Azure Data Studio
API	Application Programming Interface
ARM	Azure Resource Manager
AS	Analysis Services
ASD	Azure SQL Database
AzDO	Azure DevOps
B2B	Business to Business
B2C	Business to Consumer
BI	Business Intelligence

BIDS	Business Intelligence Development Studio
CD	Continuous Deployment
CI	Continuous Integration
DC	Domain Controller
DDL	Data Definition Language
DML	Data Manipulation Language
EG	Enterprise Gateway
ELT	Extract Load Transform
ETL	Extract Transform Load
IaaS	Infrastructure as a Service
IaC	Infrastructure as Code
IR	Integration Runtime
KQL	Kusto Query Language
MFA	Multifactor Authentication
MSA	Microsoft Account
MSI	Managed Service Identity
OrgID	Organization ID (describes an Azure Active Directory identity)
PaaS	Platform as a Service
PBI	Power BI

PBI-P	Power BI Premium (Capacity based)
PBI-PPU	Power BI Premium Per User
RBAC	Role Based Access Security
REST	Representational State Transfer (used to describe a type of programming interface)
RLS	Row Level Security
SaaS	Software as a Service
SCD	Slowly Changing Dimension
SDU	SQL Down Under
SHIR	Shared Integration Runtime
SLO	Service Level Objective
SP	Service Principal
SSAS	SQL Server Analysis Services
SSDT	SQL Server Database Tools
SSIS	SQL Server Integration Services
SSMS	SQL Server Management Studio
SSO	Single Sign On
SSRS	SQL Server Reporting Services
TMSL	Tabular Model Scripting Language
TOM	Tabular Object Model

TR	Transactional Replication
UAT	User Acceptance Testing
VM	Virtual Machine
VS	Visual Studio
YAML	Yet Another Markup Language

www.ingramcontent.com/pod-product-compliance
Lightning Source LLC
Chambersburg PA
CBHW080632060326
40690CB00021B/4897